The Cedar Surf

TRANSMONTANUS 10

Published by New Star Books
Series Editor: Terry Glavin

Other books in the Transmontanus series

The Cedar Surf

AN INFORMAL HISTORY OF SURFING IN BRITISH COLUMBIA

Grant Shilling

TRANSMONTANUS / NEW STAR BOOKS VANCOUVER

For Mary Alice and Levon Ray

Contents

Acknowledgements

Thanks to the Sadler family for sharing their time and their photo album, Steve Johnson (R.I.P.) for giving some of the limited time he had left, to Barbara Oke for her time, photos and friendship, to Dave Hadden for sharing his stories, particularly the Owen Atkey-Orca story, to Ken Gibson for the information on the building of the Wickaninnish Inn, Cam Scott at coastalbc.com for the use of the glossary, and to Brian Nash for the Ply Plan Surf-board pamphlet. Thanks also to Chris Arnett for some of the canoe-surfing information, to all the people I interviewed and to Terry Glavin, Rolf Maurer and Melva McLean at New Star Books for making this book possible. And thanks to Ralph Tieleman for the Muffs board. Finally, thanks to Mary Alice and Levon Ray for sharing the wave. I'm glad I caught a ride with you.

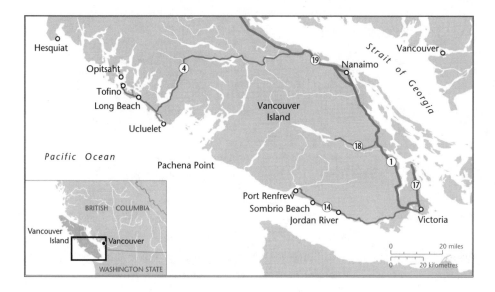

Hesquiat

Opitsaht

Tofino

Long Beach

Ucluelet

Pacific Ocean

Pachena Point

Vancouver
Island

Strait of Georgia

Vancouver

Nanaimo

19

18

1

17

Victoria

Port Renfrew

Sombrio Beach

Jordan River

14

BRITISH COLUMBIA

Vancouver
Island

Vancouver

WASHINGTON STATE

0   20 miles

0   20 kilometres

Out of the Woods
and Into the Water

Surf is a resource that can't be taken from us. If you could harvest it, it wouldn't be here. It would have been gone. They would have moved in and took it all long ago.

—BILLY LEACH, UCLUELET-BASED SURFBOARD MAKER

Enormous log trains . . . chuff seaward . . . over trestle bridges and through canyons till they hit the pier of the dumping ground that jutted like a finger from the roaring beach. The logs are spilled with a crashing sound as great as any wave. One trainload of logs was sufficient to keep a good-sized booming crew jumping for some time.

The boom men took care of the aquatic end of the business. It was a prerequisite of this job to be nimble on their feet, for you were fated to spend a good deal of your working day leaping from log to floating log, some of which were prone to roll violently or sink away from under you.

— FROM *THE HILL TO THE SPILL* BY PETE TROWER

I fancy that these boom men were British Columbia's first surfers.

Or how about this?

The first British Columbian surfer chopped down a cedar and rode the screaming tree on an endless, renewable wave.

Or this?

In 1948 Jim Sadler rode in on a horse. Sadler, the crazy bugger, rode that horse through jack pine and scrub and all kinds of wood and wheat, from Olds, Alberta to Victoria, BC. It took him two months and three days. By 1965 he was surfing Pachena Bay, near Bamfield on the west side of Vancouver Island. Wearing a diver's suit for protection against the cold, Sadler's used a 13- by-2-foot plywood surfboard with rounded edges.

Sadler may not have been the first BC surfer but he was one of the originals. The idea for writing a book about surfing in BC started with a visit to him in the early 1990s. Frank Harper, the editor and founder of *The Sound* newspaper in Tofino, suggested I go talk with Jim, a carpenter who was building affordable housing through his church for its members. I heard that he surfed and flew ultra-light airplanes that he built himself. There weren't a lot of people surfing in Tofino then, just a handful. Within a decade there would be over eighty local surfers, and thousands of surf tourists contributing to the local economy.

Surfers on Long Beach, Vancouver Island in the mid-1960s. PHOTO COURTESY OF RUTH SADLER

Sadler was the antithesis of the surfer image: religious, elderly, and, for all appearances, basically uncool. He broke the mold, and I hope this book, too, helps break that surfer-image mold created by the Hollywood B-movies inspired by California's beach culture, beginning with 1959's *Gidget*.

This is British Columbia. Just try surfing at the mouth of Juan de Fuca Strait in a bikini, like Gidget. You need a wetsuit to surf here. Clayoquot Sound, where surf town Tofino is located, can get four metres of rain a year, and the waves here are best in the wintertime. The "cedar surf" is about relative isolation, and it's about places such as Tofino, Ucluelet, Jordan River and Sombrio Beach. The cedar surf is an imaginary and a very real landscape, a warp and a weft of roads, trails, hitchhikers, squatters, "brush apes," and stories worlds apart from Los Angeles and San Diego. Tofino's year-round population of a thousand people would barely fill a 1960s-era Sunset Boulevard nightclub.

Before 1956 Tofino and Ucluelet were their own islands on Vancouver Island because there was no road through the sawtooth Mackenzie Range mountains and across Sutton Pass. You got in and out on the coastal ship *Princess Maquinna*, which served the entire west coast of Vancouver Island. Cedar-surf pioneers like Sadler wore awkward wetsuits and lived in cedar-shake shacks on the beach and surfed waters no one had ever surfed before. And they surfed alone. The beaches here were crowded with sea lions and eagles, not people.

After 1956 there was a dusty, dirty and dangerous logging road, and in 1964 MacMillan-Bloedel Ltd. and fellow forest-company giant, BC Forest Products Ltd., built Highway 4 in exchange for logging concessions from the provincial government. The environmentalists and the surfers among the million or so visitors to Tofino and Ucluelet every year owe it to those logging companies for getting them out of the woods and into the water.

Another major focus of surfing on the BC coast lies to the southeast of Tofino and Ucluelet, where you'll find Jordan River and Sombrio Beach. The beaches there are more readily accessible from Victoria, but they're also part of the story of old-growth rainforest logging, an industry that dominates the landscape to this day. The area remains relatively unpopulated. The land has been clearcut. Some of the biggest cedar trees ever felled in Canada came from the forests behind those beaches.

Cedar was also the economic basis for the first peoples of this coast. Carved into houses, cradles and coffins, with its inner bark woven into robes, mats and hats, cedar was also what got the Nuu-chah-nulth peoples out on the water. For the T'Sou-ke, Ditidaht and Pacheenaht, as well as the Tla-o-qui-aht, Ahousaht, Hesquiaht and Ucluelet, *hobis*, the western red cedar, was easy to split and carve and was particularly well suited for making the great ocean-going canoes for which they became world famous. From those canoes they fished, hunted whales, traded over long distances, and made war. And while the Nuu-chah-nulth lived on the water, they didn't "surf" *per se* — perhaps the water was too cold — but they practiced a form of "canoe-surfing," both for pleasure and out of necessity. It's what you have to know how to do to land a canoe on a beach in rough water.

When he was a boy, Chief Charlie Jones, hereditary chief of the Pacheenaht people, used to joyride canoes and "surf" them in, hitting the beach dead on and splitting the bow of the pirated craft. The proper technique was to surf in, turn the stern slightly near the end of the ride and let the sea turn the canoe and wash it up on shore. The term for the manoeuvre was *paqw'eiyab*. If the canoe hit the beach and stopped, it was *paqw'est*. If it turned crosswise, and a following wave washed it up on the beach, it was *paqw'esedabt*.

Joe Martin of Opisat is a traditional Clayoquot carver, as is his brother Carl. Joe recalls "canoe surfing" near Hesquiat, at the far tip of Clayoquot Sound, sometimes standing in the canoe, and sometimes sitting. "We'd surf until the canoe broke," he laughs, "and then we'd get another one. It gave us something to do."

The cultural origin of contemporary surfing lies in ancient Polynesian traditions, particularly those of the Hawaiians. Captain James Cook was the first European to record observations of surfing in Hawaii. Cook and his crew of non-swimming sailors were confronted by the curious sight of brown naked bodies riding planks of wood as long as six metres and weighing close to ninety kilograms. Cook wrote:

> Whenever, from stormy weather, or any extraordinary
> swell at sea, the impetuosity of the surf is increased to
> its utmost heights, they choose that time for this

amusement: twenty or thirty of the natives, taking each a long narrow board, rounded at the ends, set out together from the shore.[1]

In 1778 Cook became the first European to set foot in what is now British Columbia, at Friendly Cove on Vancouver Island's northwest coast. The BC coast's Hawaiian connections are at least as old as the earliest days of European exploration and the maritime sea-otter trade, when most China-bound ships stopped in Hawaii. At one time, a quarter of the workforce at BC's Hudson's Bay Company's coastal forts was Hawaiian.[2] Who knows? Maybe a few Hawaiian settlers took breaks from their fur-trading routines to see what our waves were like.

In 1820 the first missionaries to Hawaii were dismayed to see Hawaiian men, women and children drop their tasks to ride the waves. To god-fearing, work-oriented Calvinists, there was nothing to be gained from the Hawaiians' happy hours of self-indulgence. The arrival of these missionaries marked the initiation of a "cultural revolution" — read cultural genocide — during which surfing was denounced as an idle activity that stood at odds with Calvinist notions of piety, self sacrifice and, in general, an avoidance of anything that spelled f-u-n.

The US annexation of Hawaii in 1898 brought a new type of *haole* — white person — to the islands. These new visitors were tourists, a part of an emerging cultural ethos that celebrated nature, health, physical activity, and outdoor adventure. They were not unlike today's "eco-tourists" who seek out physical adventure with a surfing or kayaking lesson in Tofino.

Jack London played a part in the Hawaiian revival of surfing when he wrote "A Royal Sport: Surfing in Waikiki." The popular story was published in the October 1907 edition of *The Lady's Home Companion* and again in 1911 as part of the book, *The Cruise of the Snark*. In his article, London wrote:

> Where but the moment before was only the wide desolation and invincible roar, is now a man, erect, full statured, not struggling frantically in that wild movement, not buried and crushed and buffeted by those mighty monsters, but standing above them all, calm

1. Marcus, Ben. "From Polynesia With Love: The History of Surfing from Captain Cook to the Present." wwwsurfingforlife.com/history.html

2. Koppel, Tom. *Kanaka: The Untold Story of Hawaiian Pioneers in BC and the Pacific Northwest.* Vancouver: Whitecap Books, 1995.

and superb, poised on the giddy summit, his feet buried in the churning foam, the salt smoke rising to his knees, and all the rest of him in the free air and flashing sunlight, and he is flying through the air, flying forward, flying fast as the surge on which he stands. He is a Mercury — a brown Mercury. His heels are winged, and in them is the swiftness of the sea.[3]

3. Marcus, "From Polynesia With Love."

The story of surfing on North America's west coast officially begins in 1907 when Henry Huntington brought over Waikiki surfer George Freeth — of Hawaiian royalty and Irish descent — to use in a publicity stunt for the opening of a railway to Huntington Beach, California. Still, it wasn't until the late 1950s and early 1960s that surfing triggered any major cultural or commercial activity on North America's Pacific shores.

The big boom then was in California's beach towns. Now, something similar is happening on Vancouver Island's west coast, in communities where the logging and fishing industries are on the wane. Everybody sees tourism as a major contributor to current and future economies. The many surfers around provide the service industries with a cheap labour force. Also, there is more tourist money floating around, more surf schools, more leisure activity, and more non-extractive uses of "wilderness."

The Cedar Surf celebrates the distinctive aspects of a made-in-BC surfing phenomenon. Surfers in BC are carving out a unique cultural terrain in the cold water of the North Pacific, and transforming traditionally resource-based towns into places for recreation.

It's also about just "doing the fun."

Cedar Surf Safari

Jake and I are driving Highway 14 north from Victoria on the west side of Vancouver Island, towards the Jordan River and Sombrio Beach, on the lookout for roof racks and boards. It's Saturday; the car radio lets us know that the Vancouver Canucks are at home doing what Canadians do best, playing hockey. The rain is pelting down, and I keep wiping foggy breath from the windshield and noting the dirty snow at the side of the road. We are driving deep into the shivering heart of surf country.

The first stop will be the Jordan River. A snaky one-and-a-half-hour drive from Victoria, the Jordan River is a flat spot on a wide curve that has been logged down to dirt. A logging railway once stood on the hill overlooking town, and ruins of it can be seen in the Jordan River. The river was dammed in 1913 and until the mid-1950s supplied most of the power for southern Vancouver Island. To this day, tug booms regularly haul rafts of logs down the river.

The town of Jordan River consists of a restaurant, a trailer park, a roadside motel, and a Western Canada Forest Products stockyard full of cut trees. But the most important things about Jordan River, as far as surfers are concerned, are the clean waves, the point break, and river mouth break. The gradual accumulation of sand and gravel that comes down the river is mediated by rain and wave action and occasionally causes a sand bar to form at the mouth. When this happens, the surf there becomes that much better because the sand bar acts like a reef break. Every couple of years, however, the logging companies run a Cat down at low tide and remove the sand bar, piling up dirt near the point break so the water is deep enough for the tug booms to take out the boomed-up logs.

The Jordan River is the first place along Highway 14 that surfers check out. If the surf is up there, and the wind is offshore holding up the waves, most surfers will not drive the extra twenty minutes farther north to Sombrio and its winding logging road down to the beach.

When Jake and I arrive at Jordan River, there are two vans parked by the side of the road; the drivers are looking out at the waves. Describing waves is an essential aspect of surfing. It's part Zen and part physics. These surfers are looking for "mackers," aka "ground swells" — well-formed and powerful waves formed over great distances, perhaps from as far away as the Bering Sea.

For surfers and fishermen alike, the day starts with the marine broadcast. Some gale up in the Queen Charlotte Islands may become a mysterious force that works its way down the coast. All day, surfer kids drive up and down the coast to check the surf, and time becomes a giant wave of building energy. It's a crazy multiplying energy — the bigger the wave the greater the "stoke" (yes, just like wood feeding a fire) — and the need to get to the beach, to climb into the surf, to leave the land behind.

The energy of the ocean works its way into the car and the coffee and conversation. It wraps itself around the marine broadcast and the dull, neoprene smell of salty wetsuits. Jake feels the waves are closing out way too fast for there to be much good surfing. He says the waves aren't "sectiony" — long waves that have common characteristics and timing.

Jake took up surfing two years ago. He went into a store to buy a skateboarding magazine and bought a surfing magazine instead. When he went into a surf shop in Victoria, they told him his options for surfing in BC were Tofino and Ucluelet, or closer to home at Jordan River and Sombrio Beach. Along with two friends he rented a board and a suit, drove out to Sombrio and has been going out regularly ever since.

In British Columbia the best surfing is in the winter when storms make for bigger waves. In fact, wintertime is really the only time you can reliably surf Sombrio or the Jordan River, both of which depend on winter storms for surfable waves. Come summer there is only a one- or two-degree increase in water temperature. To protect against the cold you have to don five-millimetre-thick neoprene wetsuits, gloves, booties, and a devil-and-the-deep-blue-sea fanaticism. (Surfers bring an almost religious zeal to their pursuit.)

A greater risk than getting cold is getting "slammed" by a wave and having the wind knocked out of you, getting "washing machined" or "stuffed" — driven under the water by a wave coming down on you and having to wait to catch your breath. The weight of water falling on your head, when you get caught by the lip of a three-foot wave, is about 800 kilograms. Such an experience can be "hiddie" — hideous, and is sure to test your "pucker factor" — your ability to relax while waiting to catch an intimidating wave.

A huge wave in Tofino, a real "macker" would be ten feet (or overhead as it is commonly called), with an average wave about three-to-five feet high. Most waves at Sombrio or Jordan River are in the three- to five-feet range. Both Sombrio and the Jordan River provide consistent waves. The surf at Tofino is a "beach surf" — ever changing. One of the things that makes the surfing at Tofino a real challenge is the amount of paddling you have to do — "duck diving" under waves before you can actually attempt to catch one. The waves at Jordan River are formed by a point break — waves that form in reaction to a landform and are, therefore, consistent. The waves at Sombrio Beach are formed by a reef break, which also produces consistent waves.

Winter or summer, the water is icy cold at Sombrio and the Jordan River, a shrink-wrapping cold of five to six degrees Celsius. The water at Tofino, on the other hand, is a relatively balmy eight to eleven degrees Celsius. Jordan River is especially cold because of the river outflow and the snowmelt from the hills above. You can freeze your butt off out there. (Please note: Dr. Peter Amschel has proven conclusively that straddling a surfboard in very cold water causes the gonadal tissue to shrivel [duh!], thereby stimulating and increasing testosterone levels. This actual scientific research may explain better than anything why male surfers continue to surf in the cold — for the testosterone dammit!)

Heading into the surf at Sombrio Beach. Note the tri-fin board.
PHOTO COURTESY OF BRIAN HOWELL

Cold water on the skin not only feels uncomfortable, it can quickly cause the body to stop functioning. The fact that water conducts heat away from the body thirty-two times more rapidly than air means that submersion in cold water can cool the body's core temperature very quickly. You may be covered from head to foot in five millimetres of a second silicon skin, including a hood, but that leaves your face the most vulnerable part of your body. You want to avoid putting your head underwater because your body loses about half its heat through your head. Special receptors all over it are linked to the "aquatic mammalian diving reflex," which gives you that breathless feeling when cold water hits. You are also likely to get one of those "ice cream" headaches.

If you start feeling cold while surfing in the winter, you rarely warm up again until you're out of the water. Surfing is an activity requiring strenuous physical effort, and this means you can quickly enter a vicious cycle of energy and heat loss, one that makes you colder and colder. The cold makes you tired, and physical activity makes you cold. Mild hypothermia causes an increase in pulse rate, blood pressure and cardiac output, meaning that the colder you get, the faster you burn up energy. Burning energy, in turn, makes your body cool down much quicker. So if you get hypothermia you should rarely try and swim to safety because doing so will make your body cool down up to thirty-five percent faster. Staying still and waiting for rescue is probably the safer bet.

Looking at the unsurfable waves leaves Jake and I time to sit in the car and talk. I ask him if he ever heard of Jimmy Hilborn, and when he says no, I tell him Hilborn's story.

On December 27, 1974, a picture of a surfer at Jordan River appeared on the front page of the *Victoria Times-Colonist*. Victoria resident Jimmy Hilborn, who was 17 at the time, saw the photo and said to himself "Wow, that looks like fun." Hilborn, a fully qualified scuba diver, owned a wetsuit and knew a guy who had a homemade hollow surfboard. He borrowed it and, two days later, went out with four friends to surf Jordan River. The plug was missing from the hollow board so he took some cardboard, wadded it up, and used it as a plug.

When they got to Jordan River there were a few people out surfing in ten-foot-high waves. Hilborn managed to get outside and off the point behind the river mouth, but then he got stymied because he didn't know how to catch waves. Being December it got dark pretty quickly and all the other guys who had been out surfing came in. They were in the sauna getting changed. Nobody paid attention to a kid who was out surfing by himself.

That was about 4 p.m. At about 8 p.m., with it pitch black and with winds building up to sixty-five kilometres an hour, Hilborn found himself struggling to keep afloat in twenty-foot troughs. He had to make sure he didn't get caught underneath the waves. To make matters worse, the freezing cold water was getting caught up under the back flap of his wetsuit. He had sense enough not to waste his energy and lose body heat. He just lay on his board in the dark. He also became aware that his hollow board was disintegrating.

When a westerly came up and blew him all the way to Sooke, Hilborn began to think about his loved ones and who would be at his funeral. It was while Hilborn was picturing his own funeral that a log hit him. He held onto both the log and his board as best as he could. The log turned out to be a miracle because thirty minutes after it appeared Hilborn's board sank. He knew he couldn't stay on top of the log because it kept rolling in the sea. A bit farther on, he found another log. It had kelp on it. Hilborn used the kelp to lash the two logs together. The wind, however, kept getting stronger, and Hilborn was unable to stay on top of the logs. He was forced to go into the water and hold onto the logs. By this time, helicopters, fishing boats and the Coast Guard cutter, *Racer*, were raking the ocean and the shoreline. The helicopters flew over Hilborn twice that night with their searchlights on but couldn't spot him because of the black wetsuit and the black toque he was wearing.

After a night of this, and now into the next day of his nineteen-hour ordeal, Hilborn knew he had to find something more secure. In the middle of a kelp bed, he found another log that he knew would hold him up. He was on the log, about a half a kilometre from Secretary Island, when he heard the sound of a boat and, with his remaining strength, popped out of the water and waved. Sports fishermen Bob McMahon and Jim Maulding were spring salmon fishing in their boat out of Sooke Harbour. They were on their last turn, just about to head back in when they happened to look in Hilborn's direction.

After Hilborn was rescued, his friends went out and bought him an orange toque.

Then, as Jake reminds me, there's the story of Owen Atkey's encounter with a killer whale.

Atkey, a very experienced surfer, was sitting on his board waiting for a good set at Sombrio Beach. He was surfing alone, picking only the best waves, and having a great session. At the same time, a large male killer whale was working its way westward, surfacing to breathe every few minutes, maybe looking for something to eat, homing in on any movement he could sense in the water around him. Owen knew nothing of the Orca. He was concentrating on the wave sets approaching from the west.

Owen spotted the tall dorsal fin when the whale was about a half kilometre away. Although he knew there had never been an authenticated attack on humans by a wild Orca, he noticed his heartbeat increasing. Nervously he paddled off the reef a bit. The whale kept its course, heading his way.

The whale circled around and cut off Owen's escape route to the beach. The two made eye contact. The Orca leapt from a distance of thirty feet. Most of its body was up in the air, hanging momentarily against the sky. It came down on Owen Atkey with its mouth wide open. He expected to die but he felt no fear, just anger. He thought if the whale was going to get him it would have to eat a surfboard first so he rolled off his board, grabbed it, and thrust it towards the whale.

Then, in mid-air, as if it realized its mistake, the whale rotated and arched to the left. Owen thought the pectoral fin would hit him hard, but it barely brushed his board. Turbulence from the whale's thrusting flukes spun him around and tore the board from his grasp. The whale leapt once more, heading away, then disappeared.

Jake nervously pulls down on his own toque and tries to focus on the wave conditions outside our foggy windshield. With very little wind and a small swell, there isn't much to surf so Jake and I push on to Sombrio, trying to put the scary surf stories behind us.

In the parking lot at Sombrio are about a half dozen cars. A group of surfers, most in their early twenties, are in various stages of undress, slipping into or out of wetsuits or kneeling down to wax their boards. The wax provides better foot and belly grip for paddling out to and riding the waves. Boards can be divided into two broad categories — shortboards — about five to nine feet long and longboards — aka "tankers" — over nine feet.

There is a direct relationship between age and the length of board. Most young people ride shortboards because they are easier to manoeuvre and to carve waves with. The activity resembles skateboarding; it's a bit more hot-doggy, a younger person's test of raw athleticism. Longtime longboarders are traditionalists, a strange and cultish bunch who ride big boards presumably for the same reason that people drive big cars — because they can. The longboard ride is long on elegance and short on swerves.

Some of the cold-water tribe in the parking lot jog in their wet-

Surfers trying to warm up on Sombrio Beach. PHOTO COURTESY OF
BRIAN HOWELL

suits to create some heat before they hit the water. The mood is friendly here with real *ésprit-du-boards*. A short walk from the parking lot through the clearcut and the thin remaining stand of ancient hemlock and one arrives at the pebbly beach. There are fifteen surfers bouncing up and down in the surf looking like seals among the heavy accumulation of bull kelp. In the distance are Cape Flattery and the Olympic Peninsula. Several fires burn on the beach, some with surfers huddled around them.

In 1995 twenty-something Joanne Fraser lived on Sombrio Beach for six months when it was still a squat community. Fraser moved from Victoria to Sombrio to be closer to nature and the ocean. Since then the squat community has been dismantled, but Fraser, who now lives in Sooke, has become addicted to surfing and coming to Sombrio.

"I'm here at least once a week but sometimes three or four times a week," she says, shivering in her neoprene wetsuit while sitting on a huge beached cedar log. Fraser usually drives out to Sombrio alone, although she knows many of the surfers on the beach. Today, Fraser is the only woman surfing, a fact that doesn't bother her. "Sometimes learning how to surf is intimidating for girls," says Fraser. "Surfing is not something you can pick up right away. So if there are a lot of guys out there who know what they are doing, it can be scary."

Fraser says the number of women surfing has increased in the three years since she started surfing and says, "Sometimes it's only girls out there." Generally, Fraser feels there isn't much of a competitive attitude among surfers, just a shared camaraderie of the total body rush that catching a wave can bring. When I ask her what is it about surfing that causes her to brave freezing cold waters, she pauses for some time. Her answer is almost Zen-like and reflects the crazy calm that surfing induces: "You get fresh air, some wind on your face, it forces you to take deep breaths and it makes you look at the elements different. It gets you right into the rain. Other people are sitting inside when it's raining saying 'This is lame.' But when you get right into it, it's fun."

Farther down the beach, a group of surfers up from Victoria for the day has gathered around a small fire. They have just emerged from the water, and two go hustling off to their car to turn on their heaters and change into warm clothing. A surfer in a neoprene suit jogs by them, trying to build up some heat before he plunges into the icy water. Two surfers have been surfing without their neoprene gloves and are pouring steaming hot water from a Thermos onto their hands, trying to flex some life back into their joints. They have brought a picnic spread of veggie dogs, fruit and cookies and enjoy an easy, warm camaraderie characteristic of most surfers. The sport seems to leave a healthy glow that creates a real openness.

"I don't know what it is," says Gord, 22. "Usually when you step out of the water you've had a really good time. And two hours later you've still got the smile. And so you know you've got to go out and do it again. With myself I find that if I haven't surfed in a week or so, I get a little grouchy. I miss it and I have to get back to it."

For many, the sport becomes a lifelong pursuit.

"With surfing you can't know the playing field ever," says Val Litwin, a University of Victoria English major who comes out to Sombrio as often as he can. "It is the hardest sport I've ever attempted. Other than windsurfing or sailing, it is the only sport where the medium moves with you. Nothing is constant about surfing: the wind, the tide, the current — you even have to watch out for sea lions."

Another attraction of surfing is the freedom.

"There's no lift tickets, just an initiation fee, I suppose," says Gord of the approximately one thousand dollars it costs for a board and suit.

A former biker-gone-surfer states his attraction. "There are no cops. No authority. It's one of the last things in the world you don't have to register for, and you don't need a helmet."

While some surfers buy into the renegade attitude of surfing, generally that isn't the case. "I think there is a lot of hype around it," says Fraser. "I think it's because in BC it's a relatively new surfing scene. We are our own thing, not some California scene from the '50s or something. I guess it's like anything, people get the clothes, the attitude and lingo — but it really is just a case of doing the fun."

Jim Sadler at Pachena Bay

James Sadler is a man of energy, spunk and faith. The stepping stones for his faith were laid when he came out west on a horse he rode from Olds, Alberta to Victoria in 1948. "It took me two months and three days," says Jim, 68, outside the home he built in Tofino. Jim speaks with the energized voice of an outdoorsman.

At the age of 18 he started out with $1.10 in his pocket and not enough feed for his horse. Thirty miles into the journey Sadler's horse started to canter adrift. "He was telling me something." The horse had stumbled across a field of oats. "Food for the horse was right there at our feet," he recalls.

With the horse full and content, Jim continued on his way. Just outside Banff, Sadler noticed a fellow who seemed to be blocking the road. "So I dug in and the horse sped up," Jim says. But the man still decided to reach out and grab the reins.

"'Hey,' he said. 'Do you want a job?'"

"The man's name was Brewster and he owned half of Banff. He wanted me to look after thirteen horses for him for a week. He'd pay me $25. I said, 'Could you make it thirty? 'Cuz that's what I figured I needed, eh? Brewster laughed. He said I'd get extra money from the tourists."

Jim left Banff with $65. Outside of Revelstoke he began to dehydrate. "I was real dry. The horse was drinking from these tiny puddles." And then, "Well." says Jim with a great deal of reluctance, but very much in the moment. "I looked over there," he

Jim Sadler surfing with his characteristic hand paddles. PHOTO
COURTESY OF RUTH SADLER

says indicating a spot forty years back, "and there was a crate of
purple grapes. I said 'Thank You Lord!' for turning the water into
wine."

After Sadler arrived in Victoria he settled down, married and
worked as a carpenter. He and his wife Ruth made plans to go to
New Guinea as missionaries. Jim wanted to work as a builder
there. When visa and immigration requirements caused a series of
delays Jim went to work for the Shanty Missionary Association.
The association ministered to loggers, natives, lighthouse keepers,
and prospectors throughout BC.

In the winter of 1965, Jim visited Pachena Bay near Bamfield,
where he was building a lodge. Pachena Point is legendary for its
treacherous waters. The stretch of coastline is known as the
"Graveyard of the Pacific" because of the number of ships
wrecked there. It is also the site of a lighthouse built in 1907, the
only wooden lighthouse still in operation in the province.

At Pachena Point, an Englishman gave Jim a boogie board made out of two pieces of plywood with rounded-off edges so they couldn't cut their stomachs open while surfing in the raging water. They strapped themselves to the boards with rubber tubes but their hands were free. They put on fins because Jim was an experienced scuba diver. "I took to it right away 'cuz it was so much fun," says Jim. "The English fella was kind of pissed off because he said, 'You've done this before.' And I had to explain, 'No, no I've never done this before.'"

When Sadler went back to Victoria he saw a magazine with pictures of guys standing on boards. "It made the hair on the back of my neck stand up and my palms greasy with sweat. It was just something I had to try."

That winter he built a board and brought it out to Pachena Bay. He was very frustrated for the first couple of weeks because he couldn't stand up on the board. Then he started to melt some paraffin wax on the board. He had discovered the secret of wax — it allows you to grip the board better with your feet. The board was 13½ by 2½ feet. "I mean, I had no idea," he laughs.

Sadler then came up with his own personal innovation. He made paddles out of thin plywood. Through one end he drilled a hole, took inner tubing and tied it in a loop so he could slip his wrist in with a snug fit. "Then I could grab the paddles in the middle with the fat ends on either side," says Jim. "I was knee paddling on this giant tanker and away I'd go out into the surf."

He made the hand paddles because he figured that, since he started surfing at the age of thirty-two, he needed an advantage. "I could just smoke out there with those paddles," he says.

Sadler surfed all that winter in a diving suit. Ruth, his wife, says he bulked up and put on several pounds of muscle through his shoulders and in his arms because of all the paddling he had to do.

One of Sadler's pastimes was collecting glass balls that were used as floats on Japanese fishing nets. "There used to be hordes of them. I remember going on the beach and they'd be all over, as if someone had scattered them like marbles. I loved to collect them, but so did the Coast Guard, and they would get out there with their helicopters right after a storm."

So Jim figured out how to beat the choppers. One day he loaded up his surfboard with burlap sacks, paddled out of

BC's first family of surfing, the Sadlers. Clockwise from front: Cindy, Ken, Ruth, Jim, and Harold. PHOTO COURTESY OF RUTH SADLER

Pachena Bay while a storm was just ebbing — not fully over, yet still too windy and unpredictable for the helicopters. His idea was to get in on all the beaches, collect the glass balls, and paddle home with them.

"I tried to say 'No way!'" recalls Ruth. "But Jim said, 'No, it will be fine.' So he left, and the day just went on and on and on and on, and it got dark and he still wasn't back. So I was mad and said, 'Fine, you want to go out in the storm with your stupid surf board looking for stupid glass balls, go ahead.'"

There was no electricity in Pachena Bay so Ruth hung an old kerosene lamp from the porch of the farmhouse they lived in and went to bed.

Meanwhile, Sadler was paddling back with a great sack of glass balls strapped up on top of his board. When it got dark he got sea-sick because he had no point of reference anymore. He was stuck out at the mouth of the bay until huge swells began picking him up and gradually moving him into the bay. Then disaster struck.

Jim waxing his board at Long Beach circa 1966. PHOTO COURTESY OF
RUTH SADLER

A big wave took him out from behind; his board broke and clob-
bered him. When he came up after wiping out, he had no board,
no nothing. Then, right next to him, up popped his big sack of
glass balls. He climbed up on top of the balls, wrapped himself
around them, and kept his eyes on the shore. Every once in a
while he'd get a glimpse of this light. He held on to the glass balls.
He held on, and he held on, all the while being thrashed around
in these breakers big enough to crack the hulls of ships. Eventually he was washed in and, astonishingly, made it to the beach.

Walking up the beach with his sack of glass balls, he expected
Ruth to be there with warm embraces, but the house was dark
except for that light he'd seen while he was bobbing in the waves.

Sadler's work in Pachena Bay would soon be done. He and his
family would be moving on. After his first winter of surfing there,
Sadler heard about an International Surf Contest being planned
for Long Beach, south of Tofino. It was 1966, and the contest was
the first of its kind in BC. It was made possible because of the road
that now joined Tofino and Ucluelet with the rest of the world.

Surfing in the Sixties:
Tofino, Wreck Bay and
the Wickaninnish Inn

A brochure put out by Macmillan-Bloedel in the 1960s modestly suggests: "It was the logging industry that brought Wickaninnish Bay within practical reach of the motoring public." It's true. Loggers making the run from Port Alberni to Tofino and Uclulelet brought back tales of a fabulous stretch of sandy beach so wide that you could gallop a horse, drive a car, or land a plane on it. Tofino and Ucluelet were still sleepy fishing and logging villages undiscovered by the tourist hordes, but change was in the wind.

The Wickaninnish Inn on Long Beach opened in the summer of 1964. Sitting on a spit of rock a few metres above the high-tide mark, it was named for an eighteenth-century Nuu-chah-nulth chief whose name means "having no one in front of him in the canoe." Natives would canoe surf to shore and drag their canoes from the "outside" for a shortcut across the isthmus that forms Tofino. Canoes were dragged from the beach across what is now the Pacific Rim Highway to a series of dikes and a cordwood road to the "inside" at Browning Passage. Those dikes are still there, if you know where to look.

The Inn was described in a brochure as "an improbable first-class hotel" — improbable, because in 1964 few people had heard of, let alone visited, Long Beach. A newspaper article of the day described it one of Canada's least known beaches.

Ralph Devries, 71, worked as a carpenter on the construction of Wickaninnish Inn and later stayed on as a cook. During the construction, Devries met some vacationing Californians. "I knew nothing about surfing," he says. "I had never seen a surfer before, and nobody else was surfing in Tofino or Ucluelet then. These Californians had surfboards, and I figured what the hell, why not? They showed me some of the basics."

Devries went to Victoria and bought "this real big surfboard," an extra-long longboard of 10½ feet in a pawn shop. The board, a red Malibu classic, was so big that Devries surfed without a leash for fear the board would spring back and knock him out. This meant a lot of extra swimming to retrieve the board when he wiped out.

Inspired by Devries, and perhaps anticipating the growth of surfing alongside tourism, Robin Fells, the co-owner of the Wickanninish Inn, decided to buy a few surfboards for the guests.

Naturally, the boards were used more by the young kids who were working at the hotel than by the guests. According to Devries, he had a "hell of a lot of fun" working at the hotel. He'd cook in the morning and surf in the afternoon. "The only other guy surfing there was Jim Sadler who had just arrived from Pachena Bay and he was pretty good too," recalls Devries.

In fact, Sadler was good enough to finish second in the 1966 Long Beach Surf contest in which surfers from Australia and New Zealand competed. Sadler had been surfing for a year, and by himself. "The only reason they beat me," says Jim, still full of competitive pride, "is that I got points taken off because I stayed out there too long 'cuz I didn't hear the horn. I was having too much fun and I didn't realize my heat was over."

Still waiting for their visas for New Guinea, the Sadlers decided to move to Tofino. Jim got work building the LA Grocery. Meanwhile, their children, Harold, Ken and Cindy, were "looking for something to do." Every weekend was spent at the beach.

"Surfing was about our family," says Harold, 39. "Everybody grows up playing hockey in Canada. I grew up surfing. It's just what we did. And I didn't think it was that remarkable. Until I started showing up in school with a bright red face and a wetsuit tan in the middle of December."

The Sadler boys tried to encourage others to join them. "We

worked at it but we only got a couple," says Harold. "People visiting Tofino would ask, 'What do you do out here? Well, surf, for starters,' we'd answer. And we'd get these blank, blank stares."

"My Dad put me on a board in Pachena Bay when I was three," recalls Harold, who ended up running a carpentry business in Tofino with his brother Ken, two years his junior and also an avid surfer. "I remember being panicky because it was so deep and Dad said 'Oh, you'll be fine.' He got me a small wetsuit with a little beaver tail on it. I remember him sticking me on a board, then giving me a shove, and I could stand up on this thing because it was so huge. I remember riding it and the sand going by and thinking, 'This is great!' I don't remember being scared after that."

Ken recalls, "Those were the days when you could drive on the beach. Our family would drive around. We drove up to Schooner Cove to see Jim Hudnall. Jim actually owned property overlooking the Wickaninnish Inn. They had a little cabin where we could go visit them."

"We were little kids and equipment was scarce," adds Harold. "It's not like today — now I sound like a real old-timer — you couldn't just go into a surf shop and get equipment. It took someone going down to the States, a long way down to the States, not just Oregon, but California."

Sadler built the boys surfboards designed with custom-made handles on the side. Ken recalls that the board worked great until you tried to turn with it, then it caught a lot of water and wasn't so fast. Most of the time the boys just ended up using chunks of Styrofoam seven feet long to surf on. "We would try to stand up on them, and if you could stand on those things you could stand on anything," says Harold.

Newspaper clipping from the early 1970s

The Sadler boys would spend so much time in the water that when they got out their hands were so cold they couldn't even

Surfing in winter? In Canada? You bet!

Winners of the first surf competition in 1966 at Wickaninnish. Jim Sadler, with his two trophies, is third from the left in the front row. Ralph Devries is standing far left in the back row. Notice the equal number of male and female competitors. PHOTO COURTESY OF RUTH SADLER

grab the zippers on their suits. "If Mom wasn't there we would have died because we couldn't get the wetsuits off," says Harold, laughing.

"Major hypothermia," says Ken. "I'd ask my brother, 'Can you help me?' and he'd say, 'I can't even get mine off!'"

At times Jim Sadler was there to give the boys an extra little push.

"I remember one time where Dad said, 'Okay it's time now. Grab this rope!' and basically he towed us out," says Ken.

"'Cuz we weren't strong enough," adds Harold. "He wanted us to experience catching a swell rather than just catching the foam after a wave broke. For myself, I can definitely remember the first waves that I caught that were actually swells. That was it. Game over after that. It was a totally new experience."

"Before that it was like our parents are doing something and they wanted us along so we'd go along. I remember being ticked off sometimes going to the ocean because I wanted to go to the lake. It was warm there, and we didn't have to wear a wetsuit. It really wasn't that much fun for us to play around in the water because the beach was steep at Wreck Bay, and you didn't get a long roller coming in. You got a wave that broke on the outside reef form, and it slammed down to the shore. You couldn't ride it. It was way more fun to go down to the end of the beach and spy on the lady hippies who were having a bath."

The hippies came near the end of the 1960s. They lived at Wreck Bay, just slightly north of Ucluelet, where the cliffs kept tourist trailers off the beach. To get there they had to descend a steep cliff to the Pacific and endure foot-numbing cold water. A person had to be determined. Wreck Bay served as a refuge — a giant liberation zone. The waves collapsed onto a beach dotted with driftwood, pole shelters covered with plastic sheeting, summer gypsies, hippies, draft dodgers, bohemians, families, and some surfers.

As Ralph Devries recalls, "A few of them started taking up surfing but not too many. A few other people started surfing as well. Everybody was a beginner." Devries suggests that living at a beach sounds more romantic than it was. "A lot of the hippies were miserable, especially once it started raining."

In any case, it was between those contrasting atmospheres, a first-class hotel at Wickaninnish and the liberated beach community at Wreck Bay, that the surf scenes of Tofino and Ucluelet emerged.

In 1970, when Laverne Duckmanton was working as a cook at the Wickaninnish Inn, he watched Ralph Devries out surfing and decided he wanted in on the action so he grabbed one of the Wick's surfboards. Fortunately, Robin Fells, who was Duckmanton's boss, was there to encourage him.

Duckmanton says that Fells was an extremely progressive employer. "He'd come walking through the kitchen and start looking out the window to check the surf, kind of suggesting by his gestures that maybe we should be out surfing. The next thing you knew we were all downing tools and heading into the hotel's van to go surfing. The waitresses would show up for their shifts and there'd be nobody there to cook . . . and Fells would have been behind it," laughs Duckmanton.

Duckmanton surfed in a pair of cut-off shorts and an old diving jacket with the sleeves cut off. "It was pretty chilly," he says. Leashes weren't invented yet, so surfers would drill a hole in their boards' fins and attach twine, surgical tubing or snub line from fishing trawlers, and then they'd tie the rope to their ankles. Before the invention of leashes, Duckmanton says, "You didn't want to wipe out because a swim to shore to chase your board would cost you a lot of energy."

Bruce "Bruno" Atkey, Owen's brother, was living at Wreck Bay and became a mentor to Duckmanton. "Bruce is one of the true pioneers of surfing in BC," says Laverne. "He is responsible for discovering more breaks than anybody on Vancouver Island. He is a true soul surfer."

Duckmanton went down to Wreck Bay and asked Bruce to help him get started. He bought a board from Bruce, who also gave him stacks of surfing magazines. "There were no surf videos then, so the way you learned was by watching people surf, going out there with them, and paying attention."

Duckmanton remembers going out to Twin Rivers near Ucluelet to surf with Atkey just after a logging road had been pushed through, making it possible to surf there. They drove out in Duckmanton's 1956 Volkswagen Beetle. Atkey had seen the break from the water while working on a herring boat.

Large and laconic, Atkey, 52, was born in Saskatchewan and now lives in Sooke. He built his first surfboard in "shop" at Oak Bay High School in Victoria. Atkey embodies the notion of a "waterman." Early surfers were known as "watermen," or people who had a powerful and varied relationship with the ocean — swimming, diving, fishing, boating, and beachcombing. "Watermen" lived by the ocean and had an intimate knowledge of tides, currents, and weather patterns because their livelihoods usually depended upon it.

While still in high school, Atkey built a cedar shack down at China Beach, one of a string of beaches between Sooke and Port Renfrew. "That shack was burnt down by hippies. My whole his-

tory along the coast is having shacks burnt down by hippies," says
Atkey, grouchily. He was particularly sensitive the day I visited
him. His most recent surf retreat out near Hesquiat near the outside of Clayoquot Sound had just been burnt down. Atkey's son
Ollie, who lives on Chesterman Beach with his mom, is a top
surfer on the competitive scene.

One day, coming down the cliff from Wreck Bay to surf, Laverne Duckmanton met Jeff Reves, an American dodging the
draft. Born in Santa Monica, Reves, 52, began surfing in 1961. He
recalls that the Wreck Bay scene was like nothing he had ever
seen before. "Every log on the beach at one time was used to
build someone's house," says Reves, who was dodging the draft.
Before coming to Wreck Bay, Reves spent some time in Vancouver and was probably the first person to ever surf English Bay. "I
watched for a while and saw that when the wind blew northwest
for a few days you'd get these perfect little sets. So I paddled out
and gave it a try."

Reves came out to the West Coast, worked as a logger and
camped out at Wreck Bay. He eventually bought property at Chesterman Beach. "Growing up in California, I was always trying to
get away from people when I surfed. Here I was trying to find people to surf with."

In 1973 finding someone to surf with got a little easier, courtesy
of Pierre Trudeau and the "swinging" era of the Liberals. Surfers
Doug Palfrey, Doug Harvey, Steve Ritchie, Budd Watt and Derek
Richardson got what was known as an OFY (Opportunities for
Youth) grant, which provided them with $100 a week to give free
surfing lessons at Long Beach. Their gear consisted of ten shorty
wetsuits and ten surfboards, and every morning at 10 they'd go
down and set up on the beach. They had a sign, and anyone who
came along and was interested would sit down, and one of the
surfers would give them a lecture about how waves were gener-
ated, where they came from, and why they came in sets. They
also taught a little bit about water safety. Then they'd put the stu-
dents in wetsuits, give them their boards, and away they'd go in
the water.

Jordan River

If Tofino, as a result of the new road, was slowly on its way to being discovered by hordes of tourists, Jordan River and southwestern Vancouver Island would remain the domain of logging companies and the people who worked for them. Dave Hadden was one of those individuals.

I met Dave Hadden after reading several of his stories online at www.coastalbc.com, a surfing and outdoor adventures website. Hadden, 56, is the elder storyteller in its chat forums. The forum features a lot of digital chest-beating and paranoia about media exploiting and destroying the soul of surfing, or revealing all the secret spots. Hadden lends a voice of calm reason; these concerns are the same ones he first heard expressed thirty years ago when he started surfing.

Hadden moved to Jordan River in 1974. For most of the twelve years he lived there, he was the only "local" surfer. Jordan River still has a well-earned reputation for a locals-only attitude. The funny thing is there aren't a lot of locals, just a group known as "the clubbies" who have surfed Jordan River since the late 1960s. Most of the clubbies live in Victoria and Sidney, some in nearby Sooke.

Because so few people surfed Jordan River in the early 1970s, a heightened sense of entitlement and ownership developed among the clubbies. Somehow the crown waterways at Jordan River became "their" waves. The clubbies built a cabin and sauna,

Aerial shot of Jordan River. PHOTO COURTESY OF SOOKE REGION
MUSEUM AND ARCHIVES

which became their own personal domain — a clubhouse from
which their nickname derived, although they named themselves
the "West Coast Surfing Associates." Posted in front of the sauna
was a sign that read: "Jordan River is Mine." If people outside this
small circle came to surf at Jordan River they were verbally
harassed and occasionally physically intimidated.

Members of this group would phone Hadden in Jordan River for surf reports, and if the surf was good a few of them would show up a couple of hours later from their various points on Vancouver Island. "Then I'd have to fight with them for waves!" laughs Hadden.

Localism is not unique to Jordan River. It is encountered in many surf spots around the world. What is hard to understand is why it exists in BC, where there are few surfers. Part of it might be explained by the limited "take-off" area at Jordan River — the area where you are most likely able to catch waves. Surfing, by its nature, tends to have a strong appeal to people who have small streaks of selfishness secreted somewhere within their psyches, and nowhere is it more evident than at the point on Jordan River on an inconsistent day with only a few waves per set.

Hadden has his own theory about the gnarly localism. He feels that it may be a way of trying to legitimize BC surfing by imitating the worst aspects of localism found on the beaches of California and Hawaii. "Going as far back as '75 the clubbies were always saying, 'Keep it low-key, keep it low-key.' It was always 'We'll get invaded, this is such a good wave,' or 'We don't want a big influx of Californians.' It just didn't make any sense to me that people were going to travel a thousand miles to a foreign country to steal these cold water waves from these guys," says Hadden. "I'd get stinkeye — a cold shoulder — from guys coming to Jordan River and I lived there for gosh sake!"

It's not that Hadden is completely unsympathetic. "Some guys feel they have proprietary rights to Jordan River. A few of them have been surfing there for thirty years. It's been an integral part of their psyches and it's hard to break it. The thing that dismays me a little bit is guys who have been there for only five to eight years who manifest that same attitude."

Dave Hadden now lives just south of Campbell River where he works the graveyard shift as a warehouse person, four hours from the nearest surf. Hadden's house, which he shares with his wife Susan, is a respectable suburban job in the middle of many trailer homes, tucked away on streets with the names like Sea Wave, Sea Crest, Surfside, and Dolphin Street. Hadden considers the names "pretty ironic, considering I'm a surfer, eh?" The cramped streets are a mirror of his physical condition. He suffers from nail patella syndrome, a genetic disorder that has squared his kneecaps and caused the disappearance of his fingernails. As a

A surfer "drops in" on Dave Hadden at Jordan River. PHOTO COURTESY OF DAVE HADDEN

result he can no longer surf, but he says he thinks about surfing every day.

Dave greets me at the door — a tall, thin fellow with a pleasant face and a pack of Rothmans tucked in his shirt pocket. Up on his computer screen is a picture of himself just about to catch a big wave at Jordan River. "My credentials, if you like," he says.

Hadden brings an intimate knowledge to water; his passion for surfing is matched only by his passion for salmon. A self-described "fish head," Hadden worked for many years for the Roderick Haig-Brown Society, preserving salmon streams. After much internal debate, he has decided to share some of the stories about Jordan River, something the ever protective clubbies have asked him not to do. "But," as he says, "surf storytelling is as close as I get to paddling out."

The first time Hadden surfed was in 1973 at Long Beach. He and some friends bought a 4- by-8-foot-thick piece of polyurethane foam, cut it in half, and hacked it out so they had the rough shape of a surfboard. They fibreglassed the foam boards and painted them red and white with red maple leafs, and made plywood fins with no leashes. "Pretty ugly boards, but they floated," laughs Hadden.

"I caught a wave and that was it. The surfing bug bit me big time," says Hadden. He was determined to go surfing and that determination evolved into finding a surfboard through a purchasing agent from a logging company in Vancouver.

Hadden checked out the surfing at Jordan River. "I'd never seen waves that mechanical and long and perfect," he says. He decided it was the place that he would learn how to surf, so in March 1974 he rented a trailer about twenty minutes away. By the end of April, Jim Van Dame, who owned the Shell service station in Jordan River, offered Dave the use of a cabin right near the breakers. For a brief period of time, Jim and Dave were the only other local surfers. Together they ran the service station where Shakies restaurant (named after a shake mill owned by Les Wade) now stands. Dave recalls they were pretty broke all the time, "just scuffling along." When the first swells started in September, Dave would put up a sign at the gas station that read: "I'm out surfing. If you need gas, beep or flash your lights."

Hadden says there were about fifteen or so active surfers at that time who were out to Jordan River pretty regularly, "Although seldom were they all out at once, and during the week Jim and I often had the place to ourselves or shared it with one or two of the regulars."

Jim Van Dame, a draft dodger, initially came up to Jordan River on a drive with a girlfriend. He surfed and stayed. He got his amnesty in 1975 but hung around until 1976, when he decided to go back to California. After Jim Van Dame left for good, Hadden was the only surfer who actually lived in Jordan River. For years, "Sombrio" Steve (Johnson) and "Rivermouth" Mike from Sombrio were the only other semi-locals there. "I always welcomed newcomers," Hadden says.

When Johnson started surfing at Sombrio he was alone most of the time. If he chose to surf at Jordan River, however, it was a different story. "When I first got there the clubbie guys would kind of tug on my leg as I was paddling out and say 'Hey, why don't you go surf at Sombrio. You can't surf here!' But after I surfed there awhile they got to know me and they'd invite me into their sauna at the beach there."

Peter Schulze, who started surfing twenty years ago when he was working in a fish plant in Ucluelet, had a slightly different experience. "We slowly got accepted at Jordan River, but we were still Long Beach surfers and Long Beach surfers weren't accepted

as well as the regular Victoria guys. We had better stamina and
better wave knowledge, but we didn't ride the waves as well as
those guys. One ride there is like ten of ours at Long Beach
because of the power it generates."

The wave at Jordan River is a speed wave, and if you aren't
hustling down the line you don't make it very far. Many surfers I
spoke to suggested that surfers who grew up surfing beach breaks
tended to be better surfers than those who surfed point breaks
most of the time. The former learned to read peaks, paddle for
them, go left and right, and developed a versatility that the consis-
tency of a point break doesn't demand.

For his part, Schulze adapted a strategy to eventually catch
waves at Jordan River among the clubbies. "What we started
doing was hanging down the line. All the waves that the clubbies
didn't like or couldn't grab, we'd go. Then there's a closeout spot
right in front of the sauna. That's where a section is, and we'd sit
there and wait and catch them there too."

Hadden continued to run the service station up until June of
1976. By then the self-serves had come around and effectively put
all the little stations out of business. The absence of a gas station
further contributed to the sense of Jordan River being "nowhere"
— a sense that suited the clubbies just fine.

The Jordan River Hotel, which burnt down in 1984, was everybody's living room and social centre. Another social activity was
renting surf films from California. Hadden rented the classic California surf movie *Free Ride* from Bill Delaney, the producer of
the film. "I phoned him. And I said, 'Hey, we're a bunch of Canadian surfers up here and there is no venue where we'll be able to
see your movie and I could show it to our little group.' Well, he
thought that was pretty cool." He rented it to Hadden for a nomi-
nal sum. To avoid paying any duty, Hadden brought the film up
as a surf-rescue training film. He rented a gas-powered generator
and borrowed a film projector. All the Jordan River surfers were
there, and a few surfers came down from Sombrio Beach. From
1975 until the early 1980s Doug Palfrey, Ted Goodspeed and Jeff
Reves would get together to rent surf movies like *Five Summer
Stories* and *A Winter's Tale* and put on dances. Reves remembers
it as an attempt to consolidate what was then a very small surf
community "where everybody knew everybody."

Unlike Jordan River, localism and a negative vibe have never been part of the surf scene in Tofino. It might be due to the wide expanse of the beach or perhaps because Tofino is an actual town. Jordan River was a company town, sparsely populated, where little sense of community was able to develop. It is, in a sense, unclaimed territory that a bunch of outsiders made their own. In Tofino, on the other hand, there is a sense of belonging to a community without the localism.

"Jordan River has a far more pioneering mentality than Tofino," says Ian Gurard. In the early 1990s, Ian Gurard lived part time on the Sombrio River in a cabin that he shared with a few other people. "The down-island surfing crowd is a pretty hardcore bunch of people, not in a nasty, territorial kind of way, although that was there as well, but just absolutely nothing to do with the scene. The people are there to surf because they like being on the beach in the rain and they love experiencing that West Coast thing. Not because of media hype, which Tofino has to do deal with. Tofino is a surf culture, whereas down island the surf culture was anti-surf culture, which appealed to me. I liked the whole vibe of jeans and Mack jackets versus Quiksilver outfits and all the right shit and the right shoes," says Gurard, laughing,

Gurard feels that if it's too crowded at Jordan River or Sombrio there is always somewhere else. "The wonderful thing about living in BC is if you are up for it there is always a little bit farther to go. We do live in one of the last places in the world where there is still uncharted surf or surf that doesn't get surfed on a regular basis — areas where you can camp and be by yourself or with your friends and catch quality waves. These places are work to get to, but they are out there. And they don't even exist in other places in the world where they are tracked out."

On the Beach: Sombrio and the Oke-Johnsons

The stones of Sombrio Beach fumble against each other, making the sound of clacking castanets as a wave gently rakes over them. The fist-sized stones, left over 15,000 years ago by glaciers, have been worn smooth by the endless weight of water wearing down the rock into pebble and eventually sand. The play of light on water suggests a spirit's presence. On the horizon the Olympic Peninsula marks traces of the western slopes.

Just above the beach, in the trees, is a dwelling, a cedar-shake shack. A wood stove is puffing out smoke into the morning mist. A hand-carved cedar paddle leans against the shack just outside the door. There is a loft with a window covered by a sheet of plastic. In front are plastic buckets for scooping water from the river. Beside the shack, set between two hemlocks, is a "gun rack" of longboards. On a sawhorse sits a child's shortboard. Chickens scratch at the ground.

A young, red-headed girl steps out from the shack, slips on a wetsuit, and says "See ya" to her mother, who is attending to a baby. She shoos a chicken off her surfboard. A couple of goats follow her to the beach where she joins her father, sisters and brothers.

A clear, sunlit crest of a wave, fat with bull kelp, breaks as a young girl and boy paddle out to catch their first waves of the day. They will spend hours in the cold five-degree-Celsius surf. It's a day like any other day here on the beach: endless repetition of sun, wind, waves, and surf.

Steve Johnson surfing Sombrio Beach. PHOTO COURTESY OF BARBARA
OKE

Under the towering presence of hemlock and spruce, more
children move through a backyard of fern and cow parsnip to join
their mother. The tree roots reach to the earth with a centuries-old
embrace. The sky is a dream — liquid, almost sea. Hanging from
several trees over the river's shore, pungent with skunk cabbage,
are swings the children play on while their mother does laundry
in the river. From here she can see her children in the surf.

Some people believe that Sombrio is Spanish for "fine gold".
In fact, this area was sighted and named in 1774 by the Spaniard,
Juan Perez; the potential for gold and profit was behind Spanish
interest in the Pacific Northwest. In 1864 there was a short-lived
gold rush in the Sooke area, and in 1907 the largest hydraulic
placer gold-mining operation ever built on Vancouver Island was
set up at Sombrio Beach. But actually Perez's *Rio Sombrio* means
"misty river", an origin for the name that is often reflected in the
sombre mood that hunkers over the area.

Regardless, the value of this place goes far beyond any gold

The Oke-Johnson children: Leah Oke, at age 11 (top); Jesse Oke (immediately above), and Isaiah Oke, age 3, with his father's longboard at Sombrio Beach (left). PHOTOS COURTESY OF BARBARA OKE

that might be found here. For sixteen years Barbara Oke and her partner, Steve Johnson, lived on Sombrio Beach, raising eleven children in a cedar home they built themselves. Johnson arrived in 1975, starting out in a driftwood and tarp shelter. To reach the beach at that time involved a forty-five-minute hike from Highway 14 through dense forest, with a surfboard tucked under his arm. "If you wanted to get to the beach, you really had to want to get there," he says.

Now 50, Johnson sports a big silver beard and has a head of fine, silver hair pulled back into a ponytail. He is originally from Huntington Beach, California — the birthplace of surfing in North America. He came up to Canada in 1970 as a draft dodger, first landing at Wreck Bay and eventually settling around the Sooke area where he worked for BC's forestry department, made some money and did some surfing.

"When I first got to BC I hung out at Wreck Bay for three or four months," says Johnson. The first board Johnson bought in BC was a surfboard built by Tofino's Wayne Vliet. "That surfboard had a lot of meat in it," he says.

Johnson started surfing near Ucluelet where he was living at the time. "The first place I surfed up there was Wreck Bay," he recalls. Johnson lived in the bush in a "little teepee." He was travelling around the Tofino area in a dugout canoe, island hopping, trying to survive at the same time. "When I first started I had a little crappy wetsuit and a little crappy surfboard and it just didn't interest me. When I could afford it I got a better suit and board and became more interested. The surfboard I had at first couldn't even float. I was trying to stand up on this board and I was thinking, 'Uh, I'd better get a job tree planting or something.'"

Johnson notes that the biggest difference between surfing Sombrio and Tofino is the reef break. The waves at Sombrio are more powerful as a result. "Sombrio is easy for paddling, the current that is taking you out is like an escalator or something — it's pretty easy," he says.

Barbara Oke grew up in the woods on the Sooke River. "We spent our summers in the river," she says. "So living outdoors is more natural to me than trying to live somewhere where my neighbor is really close."

Barbara Oke first visited Sombrio with some friends when she was 18. She came to live there in 1982 with Steve Johnson and two children (Jesse and Dawn) from a previous relationship. They moved into "The Roundhouse," a cedar house built by squatters who had come earlier to Sombrio. The house was round, about three metres across, and had a window facing the ocean.

The Okes moved out of the Roundhouse right after their daughter Meghan was born; a tree fell on their bed two nights after Barbara gave birth. They moved farther down the beach where they built a house and set up a garden. Once every couple of weeks Johnson and family would hike the steep trail to the road to buy groceries in Sooke, about twenty-five winding kilometres south on Highway 14.

Beginning in the early 1980s, logging commenced on the steep slope that Johnson, Oke and their four children at the time hiked down to the beach. "A fellow from Greenpeace came and told me they were going to be logging here and we should do something about it," says Johnson. "But nothing happened. They just came and logged."

Over a three-year period, the loggers cleared everything along the scenic strip of forest known as area 222, Crown land which Western Forest Products had acquired the rights to log. Only a thin strip of hemlock and spruce, on a part of the property owned by the Gallop family near the beach, remained. At the end of the logging road today is a parking lot for what is now the Juan de Fuca Provincial Park.

Barbara Oke believes that there was no better place to raise children than on the beach. "Wood washed up to your door. There was fresh water in the river. The kids could spend a lot of time outdoors on the beach. They could go outside and cut down stinging nettle and cow parsnip, make birds' nests in the trees, play with baby geese and baby goats, go hop on the friendly surfers' backs, steal their hats, and play in the tidal pools. We had a house with a lot of windows, so they could be a quarter mile away and I could still see them," says Oke, whose bright red hair is evident in many of her children.

"At Sombrio I'd just be in the woods all day, going through the trees, just sitting in the sun and surfing all day," recalls Leah Oke, 15, of life at Sombrio. "I feel so lucky to have had that. It will probably help me all of my life. It leaves you a lot smarter nature-wise."

Jesse's cedar-shake cabin on Sombrio Beach. PHOTO COURTESY OF
BARBARA OKE

While there weren't any other families living at Sombrio, many people were coming and going. "There weren't a lot of families," says Leah, "but there were a lot of girls that were in their twenties. They were all my friends. Those were the people that I hung out with. That's been the case ever since I was a kid. It was good though."

Tracey Chester was one of those girls in her twenties who surfed and hung out with the Oke kids down at Sombrio Beach. She recalls going to Sombrio one Christmas with presents and everybody going out surfing and singing Jingle Bells with the kids out in the surf. She says both Jesse and Isaiah had almost mystical or intuitive understandings of the ocean. "There was this huge, downed tree that extended into the water. Isaiah would sit on that for hours, naked, and just watch the water. He'd come to the beach and say some big waves were coming way before there was any evidence of that."

Steve was the surfer to start. Then the kids picked up on it. "It was only natural," says Barbara Oke. "There are three or four surf breaks right in front of the house. They were bound to have fun out there."

Johnson's surfing companions were his family. Leah, Jessie and Isaiah were perhaps the most dedicated surfers. "Surfing with your children is special," says Johnson. "Especially as they got good. They'd paddle out and I'd be mesmerized by the moves they were pulling."

"I've been in the water all my life, pretty much ever since I could stand," says Leah. "I was in the water on a boogie board pretty early, but I actually started surfing when I was about six and a half, and could stand by the time I was seven. I could surf really good by the time I was eleven. I could surf as good as most of the riders around where I lived. I'd go every day, sometimes two, three times a day."

Leah was home schooled. "I went from grade three to grade eight and I did fine. School was not a priority at all. Surfing will always be top priority for me," she says. Last summer Leah worked for Jenny Hudnall at the Surf Sister School in Tofino. She plans on making a living from surfing.

"You can have a surf school, or you can own a surf shop or, if you are good enough, you can go for the pro tour and just travel around the world. That's what I'd like to do, just travel around the world and make money surfing — it would be just great. It couldn't be that hard to do."

Jesse Oke had established a reputation as one of the West Coast's top surfers. For Jesse, however, competition was not that relevant to surfing. He took part in a few local competitions but preferred to surf on his own a lot of the time. From the age of 15 he lived in his own house on Sombrio. He started tree planting that summer and saved money to travel and surf in Western Samoa and in Hawaii. "He didn't act like a local," says Johnson. "I think that's because he travelled a lot. If he saw a kook — beginner surfer — he'd say, 'Follow me if you can. I'll show you the ropes.'"

Chesterman Beach and the Growth of Surfing

In the early 1970s Chesterman Beach was one place for some of the Wreck Bay refugees to stay in Tofino and get on the grid. Chesterman's is a three-kilometre stretch of sandy beaches with three or four surf breaks and is a five-minute drive from the four-way stop that is downtown Tofino." People couldn't figure why anyone would want to buy property at Chesterman's," recalls Jack Gillie, 51, who moved to Tofino in 1974 and worked with Ralph Devries in the carpentry trade for fifteen years. "It was a windy beach and there was no place to dock a boat. That was their concern. It took people a while to start to live out there."

Gillie came to Tofino from Hamilton, Ontario with his brother Rick, who now lives in Sooke and surfs that part of the Island. The brothers learned how to surf on Lake Ontario on boards they made from plans they saw in *Popular Mechanics* magazine. Gillie did some surfing on the Jersey shore and in South Carolina, but nothing prepared him for Tofino. "Coming to this area was a tremendous experience. It was wild and wonderful."

Gillie thought surfing was actually going to die out in Tofino in the late 1970s and early 1980s. "Most of the people I was surfing with were getting up into their late thirties, fewer people from out of town were surfing here, and the kids living on Chesterman's weren't taking it up yet. I don't know why."

Jeff Reves remembers it that way as well. He says he tried to take his son, Spirit, surfing, but he just wasn't that into it. Cold was a factor. "He didn't get into surfing till we moved back to California," says Reves, who still owns a place at Chesterman's.

"I always thought surfing would be a great thing for a kid living in Tofino to do," says Gillie, who has no children of his own. "The place had a bit of a redneck edge at the time and surfing demands a great deal of initiative. You just can't back into it. Eventually you want to travel and surf in warm water, so you see the world and learn about other places and expand your horizons."

A giant laminated poster hangs on Peter Devries' bedroom wall. It's made from a picture of his dad, Ralph, carving waves on his Malibu classic during the 1970s. Peter says the picture keeps him stoked. Ralph gave the board — the only board he ever surfed — to Peter when he decided at age sixty-seven that he could no longer surf. The board has two big indents in it from decades of knee paddling by Ralph. Peter has surfed the board a few times, but says, "I don't know how he surfed it. It has no rocker in it or anything."

At the age of three, Peter started to boogie board (the board is similar to the swimming paddle used for body surfing). He would boogie board in front of his house on Chesterman's with his dad watching from shore or from farther out in the breakers catching waves. Eventually Peter got bored with just lying on the boogie board and started to stand on it. At the age of seven, he bought his first surfboard with money he saved from doing chores. The board cost $100, was 5'4" and perfect for learning on. Ralph remembers, "At first Peter was a bit scared of the waves, which is good. I never pushed him. He'd surf in the soup where the wave had broken. It happened in stages."

Initially Peter was too small for a wetsuit, so he could only spend limited time in the water. Soon he was using old rental wetsuits from the Live to Surf shop across the road from the beach. The wetsuits were only three-millimetres thick as opposed to the necessary five, but Peter willingly froze out in the surf.

The improvement over the years in wetsuit technology has been a real boon to surfing in BC's cold waters. Laverne Duckmanton recently was looking at a 1970s-era Body Glove wetsuit, which was state of the art at that time. It was known as the "animal suit," and Duckmanton says it "looked and felt like a bunch of tubes all glued together."

The sport of surfing globally, and specifically in BC, experienced a spike in popularity due to the crossover appeal from skateboarding and snowboarding. In the late 1980s, when the Tofino Village Council built a skateboard park in the middle of town, the downtown descendant of surfing became highly visible. When there's no swell you can skate like hell.

Duckmanton thinks the transition from skateboarding to surfing is good. "My attitude is that if you grew up skateboarding on pavement — a real city sport — and you start surfing, it turns your head around. It makes you more sensitive to the environment and how things can be ruined in it. Also, particularly in BC with the cold water and the fact that you have to wear wetsuits, surfing in the rain and the snow can be quite miserable. So surfing is a challenge. You rely on your own initiative and you have to claw for everything you can get out of it."

During the mid-1980s some of the Chesterman Beach babies started taking up surfing. As Ralph Devries, who moved to Chesterman's after Wreck Bay became part of Pacific Rim National Park, recalls, "All of a sudden surfing started picking up again." The rebirth of surfing along Chesterman's might be explained by a few factors: the improvement in wetsuit technology, the presence of parents in the water, a snowboarding and skateboarding crossover, and the presence of surf clothing and accessories and the advertising that went with them.

Whatever it was, surfers, like some mysterious return of salmon, started showing up at Chesterman's. Among the Chesterman children surfing were the Bruhwiler family — Sepp, Raph and Katherine — Jenny Hudnall and Sarah Kalkan. Raph Bruhwiler went to a surf school in California at the age of twelve and that sealed the future Canadian surf champion's addiction to surfing.

"I started surfing when I was twelve or thirteen," says Jenny Hudnall, now 26, who grew up along Chesterman's Beach and in California. "I was on a 6'2″ shortboard. That's when I actually decided I was going to surf. Catherine Bruhwiler was the one who taught me how to surf. She was the one who got me out there. She was going out surfing with her brothers all the time, so I started going surfing with her. And that was at Chesterman's. We had nothing to do all day except eat homemade French fries, sit around, and surf all summer."

Surfer waxing his board at Chesterman Beach. PHOTO COURTESY OF
BRIAN HOWELL

Hudnall doesn't recall all that many people in the water.
"When I started surfing, till maybe I was twenty, the only people
that I ever saw in the water were me and Catherine Bruhwiler,
Shelley Bauer and sometimes Sarah Kalkan, for the girls. And for
the guys, there was Raph and Sepp Bruhwiler and Jack Grieg,
Harold and Kenny Sadler, Jack Bauer, Bruce Atkey, Wayne Vliet,
Jack Gillie, and Tony Heald, who opened a little surf shop at the
Standard gas station in town. There was never anyone in the
water. We'd go surfing Rosie Bay just south of Chesterman's by
ourselves all the time. When we went out there was a pack, and
when we left there was nobody there."

Hudnall doesn't really remember how it grew. "A few guys
here and there. And then Coastline Surf Shop opened where
Storm Surf Shop is now. That was in '93 or '94 maybe. Then
some newspaper articles were written about this area, and people
started moving here to surf."

Today at Chesterman's there are many "beach babies" who
grew up with surfing. In fact, that institution of Canadian hockey
— the hockey mom — has its parallel in Tofino: the surfer mom.

Surfer moms pick up their kids, some as young as eight and nine, from Wickanninish Elementary School and drive groups of them out to the beach for a surf. "I can't imagine a healthier way to spend time," says one mother whose fourteen-year-old son is an avid surfer.

Shelley Bauer, 47, a Tofino resident and mother of two, started a surf club for kids between the ages of six and eleven through the elementary schools in Tofino and Ucluelet with the assistance of the recreation commission. "The main idea is to teach the kids safety and etiquette," she says. "It also offers the chance for kids who don't like or excel at team sports to have a completely different experience." Bauer approached several hotels and businesses in Tofino and Ucluelet for funding to help pay for the cost of the wetsuits and boards and found tremendous support. "There is an understanding out there that surfing represents a healthy way for our kids to grow up."

Where the kids will grow up is another question.

The development of Chesterman's into a beach suburb of Tofino has caused a huge increase in property values. At one time the houses along the beach were neatly tucked away into the woods. Unobtrusive and humble as possible, they were a carry-over of the hippie tradition established at Wreck Bay. Slowly this has changed. Bigger and bigger Malibu-type monster homes are becoming the norm at the beach. They serve as big-buck getaways for wealthy tourists. The children of the original Chesterman Beach families may not be able to afford property there.

The idea of property and real estate values is something that is foreign to Joe Martin. Martin's people, the Tla-o-qui-aht, have lived here for over 5,000 years.

Under a canopy of trees just behind "North" Chesterman Beach, in a thin sliver of morning light, Joe Martin carves a cedar dugout canoe on his ancestors' hereditary land. On either side of Martin's property are two symbols of an ever-changing Tofino. On one side is Henry Nolla, who remains living in the shack he squatted over thirty years ago. He pays no rent and, most days, works as he has for years — on the beach, naked, carving wood sculptures, and being content. On the other side of Martin is a $300-a-night luxury "wilderness resort" — or "weirderness resort" as the locals call it.

Nolla has been, in a sense, adopted as a living museum exhibit — an eclectic character from a bygone beach era — by the hotel's owners, a local bunch who have allowed him to remain on their property in exchange for work. Turfing Nolla, a well-loved Tofinoite, would be bad PR, so he remains, a part of all the weirdness that is Tofino, a bridge between the hippie ant trail and five-star resorts.

Farther down the beach at the south end of Chesterman's near Rosie Bay, a small squat community of younger surfers was set up in the late 1980s. Among this group was a kid named Adam Smallwood who had learned how to surf on Lake Ontario and now runs Blue Planet Surf School. In the mid-1990s, the surf squatters were given the boot to make room for "Rosie Bay," a closed-gate condo community. In three decades Tofino has gone from utopian communities on the beach to gated communities — maximum security by the sea — from liberation zones to limited-access zones. Some might argue that a parallel commercialization has affected surfing, but the freedom that surfing represents cannot be taken away.

Board Feet in Ucluelet,
Surfing Capital
of British Columbia

Turn left at the junction towards Ucluelet, away from Tofino, and chances are you'll lose the crowd, but if you're lucky and you like surfing, you'll end up at Island Rhino Surfboards, Billy Leach, Proprietor. The name Rhino derives from the surfing term to describe a board that is a "gun" — a board for big waves. The shop is beside an auto body shop in an industrial park. Above the garage-type structure that Leach built is a huge sign that declares, simply: "Surfing is Good."

Leach has been in Ucluelet since 1999, coming off of various experiences on Texada Island and Sechelt on the Sunshine Coast. It was in 1998, in Sechelt, a place normally not associated with surfing, that Leach built his first board. "I lived on Texada and I saw waves big enough to surf," says Leach, 40. "I just didn't have a clue how to build a board. I knew a little bit about wind-surf board building but I didn't know where to get a blank or anything like that. I used green boat foam, but it was way too soft. But I built a surfboard," he says pointing over his shoulder to where it hangs, a happy face spray painted on it. "Then I came out here and surfed a few times and I've just been building them ever since."

Leach lives in a motorhome parked outside the shop and figures he has to clear about $1,500 a month to make a go of things. A trained gas fitter, handyman and welder, Leach could find an

Billy Leach in his surf shop in Ucluelet. PHOTO BY GRANT SHILLING

easier way to make a living but building boards is his passion. "I now seriously build surfboards," says Leach. "I've built 270 surfboards in the last three years."

Leach is proud to live in Ucluelet and would love to post a sign at the junction between the two towns that reads "Ucluelet: Surfing Capital of BC." Ucluelet has a bit of reputation as the ugly stepsister of Tofino, logger country, home of the redneck, intent on destroying the environment for a day's pay. As Leach points out, they never mention the weather in Ucluelet on CBC; it's always Tofino.

"I like living here," says Leach who brings a real working-class consciousness to his work. "It will be good for this community if this business takes off. It really needs something. All our resources have been stripped from here. The big companies came in; they pretty much logged and fished till there was nothing left, and now the people that grew up here, the people that made Ucluelet what it is, are leaving. They have no choice. Surf is a resource that can't be taken from us," adds Leach. "If you could harvest it, it wouldn't be here. It would have been gone. They would have moved in and took it all long ago."

Leach resents the bad rap given to loggers. "I'm not down on a person if he does whatever work he can to feed his kids. There are excellent people here in Ucluelet. They're loggers and fishermen and most of those people would feed you if you were hungry. They would pick you up if you looked like you were cold," he says.

Surfing in Ucluelet is growing among the youth. "And that's a really good thing because there ain't a lot to do here," says Leach, a father. "It's one of those things that makes you feel great after you've done it. It's something for the kids to do, something other than just hanging out or watching TV. It's a wicked sport. There is not too much else that makes you feel the same. Other than playing music, I don't think there is anything else I do that is comparable."

Albert Strom grew up in Ucluelet, working at the Co-op store for twenty-three years. Strom figures there is more hype and lifestyle around surfing in Tofino than in Ucluelet. "Most of us here have to work eight-hour days rather than go surf," says Strom, who takes off work whenever the surfing is good at Twin Rivers, near Ucluelet. "Tofino has more of the surf lifestyle, where people are more likely to 'live to surf,' with work being secondary. I wouldn't mind doing that!" he laughs.

Strom recalls buying his first surfboard from the Wreckage, a funky junk shop in Ucluelet where someone working there was making boards in the back. One thing that characterized most surfers in BC in the early days was their willingness to surf practically anything, from plywood to glass-over-foam boards. With the nearest surf shops in Oregon, BC surfers had to scrounge boards any way they could. Some early surfers tried to make and shape their own boards.

One of Strom's earliest boards was made locally by Wild Island, a surf company that was started by Jack Gillie and Vern Ferster in Tofino. Gillie, a carpenter by trade, has made about a hundred boards, "more as a hobby, than with the expectation of making a living from it." These days, Gillie continues to make his own boards, but has closed up Wild Island.

In his attempt to make a business out of making and selling surfboards, Leach is taking an entrepreneurial leap of faith and

Make your own surfboard plans pamphlet put out by Council of the Forest Industries of BC in the mid-1960s.

he knows it. "People would think I'm crazy, building surfboards in Canada."

When asked what is involved in building a surfboard, Leach replies, "It's pretty standard. It's fifty-year-old technology. Glass over foam. Old aerospace technology. Nothing has changed over the last fifty years on a mass scale."

In 1930 Tom Blake received the first ever patent on a surfboard for his "Hawaiian Hollow Surfboard." Previously, the typical board of the late 1920s, according to surf historian Nat Young, "was still a solid redwood from six to nine feet long, flat bottomed, with the edges just barely turned up to the bottom side. Surfers would buy a redwood plank at the local lumberyard, take it home, chop it into rough shape with an axe, and then whittle it down with a plane and drawknife. The finished board was invariably flat, heavy and about 3½ inches thick."

World War I helped stimulate the development of waterproof glues that could effectively bond wood together. By 1935 Tom Blake was at the leading edge of innovation. He added a small fin at the bottom rear end of the boards. This allowed the surfer to pivot and turn more freely and with more lateral stability.

During the 1940s surfboard design took giant steps forward. Fibreglass, resin, and Styrofoam, the three main components of today's surfboard, came out of airplane research during World War II. Surfboards no longer had to be made out of wood.

Los Angeles was the technical centre for the war effort. It was also the home of modern surfboard revolution. In a weird way, the "war effort" contributed to the creation of the ultimate pacifist and future counter-cultural icon: the surf bum.

As surfing grew in popularity in the 1950s, individuals began to develop personal techniques that became incorporated into surfboard design. There has always been a bit of the chicken and the egg with board design and performance. Did the board make it possible? Or, did the surfer push the board design?

Over the last twenty years, a whole set of new words and phrases to describe surfing has emerged because of the development of shorter boards and the use of skateboard-like moves. Phrases to describe floaters and airs like Ollies, pop-shove-its, frontside grab airs, frontside stalefish-to-tail blunt, backside method grab stomp, frontside roast beef grab, fakies and the rodeo clown were unknown twenty years ago. Hot-dogging in the 1960s and 1970s meant "nose-riding" — walking up and down the board.

The end of the 1960s saw the beginning of the shortboard revolution. Surfboards became three to four feet shorter, making them more sensitive to design details and changing their performance on the waves. Experiments in fin and tail shapes took place in the dusty shops of surfboard makers and eventually emerged in the 1970s and 1980s as twin fins and tri-fin thrusters. In fact, the tri-fin setup became standard in the 1980s and gave the drive and maneuverability needed for shortboard design to reach another level.

By the beginning of the 1990s, surfboard shapers began shaving down volume and outline to make highly sensitive boards — perhaps too sensitive, according to Billy Leach.

"I build really strong, durable surfboards," he says proudly. "The reason being is that they are made out of petroleum products. I can't, with a clear conscience, build something that may be a pound lighter, that is going to last half the time just so some guy can go out and vainly fly in the air or something. Personally, I won't do it! I don't think so! It used to be bad if you went out and broke your surfboard in half. Now it's cool. People need to change their attitude. Three hundred bucks worth of petroleum products that is headed for the dump? That is not cool. I don't consider myself a huge environmentalist or anything like that. It's just common sense. You hit a certain point of wave to strength, where you go too far. The same thing happened with mountain biking. You've got people coming in for these $90 titanium bolts to shave two ounces off the weight of their bike, and you're looking at them thinking, 'Man, go ride the thing and shave ten pounds off your ass!'"

Leach also believes it is possible to make good wooden boards like they did in the early days. "My friend built a wooden board a year ago," he says. You should see this slab. It's cedar. He surfed and it was amazing. It was about seven feet long, narrow, kind of gunny-shaped. It was like an inch and a half thick and had an inch of rocker in the thing."

Due to the larger market and increased demand for surfboards in California, there is a division of labour there that doesn't take place here. "It's easier in California," says Leach "because you know I wouldn't be glassing and sanding and all that. I would just shape surfboards. Down there it's a few different trades. Up here you ain't got a lot of options. You just do it all."

In order for Leach to make a good go at surfboard building, he has to do the impossible: build 10,000 surfboards a year. To make a little more money Leach plans to sell his own boards out of his shop in Ucluelet. "I build a little better board. I charge a good price and I only build a hundred boards a year. And I can sell that easy, because I've got a good reputation for building good boards."

Leach is also gearing up to make 10,000 skateboards a year and market them into the US. "We have a pretty innovative product, and our cost is there because we use different materials," he says. "I find with any of these industries, if you just start using the same materials, building exactly the same product, where is the edge? It's not because you buy cheaper material. You're competing with big corporations for the same material. We use different material. Different processes that are a little more flexible, easy for us to tool up, we build our own equipment."

Meanwhile, Leach is waiting for capital to make a go of things. In a dying resource town like Ucluelet you'd figure it would be easy for Leach to receive government funding to build his plant. Guess again.

"They look at me and think, okay, he must be making money. I had a hundred grand in the bank. I capitalized myself. I could've just went and sat on the beach. But I love what I do. I love to build surfboards. I'd like to see better boards built, and built here in Ucluelet."

A Luau at the Legion? In Tofino?

Hu! Kai Ko'o Loa (Well up raging surf!)

—TRADITIONAL HAWAIIAN SURF CHANT

Was it mushy? Or was it poohey?
Or was it mushy-poohey?

— TOFINO SURF TALK

The Royal Canadian Legion Clayoquot Branch No. 65 in Tofino looks out on Lone Cone, an extinct volcano on Meares Island that gives the event a Hawaiian-tinged backdrop. Meares is the ancestral home of the Tla-o-qui-aht and Ahousaht First Nations. Opitsaht, a native village with a population of about two hundred, lines a beautiful south-facing sand beach on Meares. The lights of the houses form a distinct line at night that are visible from the Legion. Staring out from Opitsaht is a totem pole. On the totem is the personification of D'sonaqua, the wild woman of the bush who came from the moon to the ocean and up the rivers into the forest. She holds beneath her breasts a platter of serpents that contain the power, the force of the sea, a force with which the surfer tries to live in harmony.

Surfers and partygoers have gathered at the Clayoquot Legion as part of Surf Jam 2000. Forget surf guitars, the endless wave music here is rave music — a music that, like the ocean, suggests we are all connected. The set up for the next two days will play endless, ambient, one-world surf music over enormous speakers as part of the sea and sand circus that has been arranged for the competition. At first the scene is a bit jarring, a flashy, catered affair with booths for names of more products than you thought possible. The booths and the scene create an out-of-town feel. Many local surfers take part while others, soul surfers who see competition as taboo, stay away.

While Billy Leach may wish for Ucluelet to be the surf capital of BC, for now it is apparent that the title belongs to Tofino. Surf Jam sure packs some economic benefits. Gathered at The Pod, a busy coffee shop in Tofino, are surfers, geoduckers, a retired wharfinger, real estate agents, whale watching guides, and bush daddies who mingle, providing a visual cross section of the changes that have taken place in Tofino. "Ten years ago," says a former crab fisherman, "if there was one pretty girl in town, it was a miracle. With surfing, this town has become the home of surfer babes."

Bodacious babes and hunky guys (*Playgirl* did a photo shoot here) beat angst anytime. Ten years ago Tofino watched its fishing industry die and its forests embraced by mostly urban environmentalists. Land values began to skyrocket. Cedar shacks were replaced by houses straight out of any suburb. Whales became a tourist attraction. Things were a little bit serious, dude.

Today, the surfers in Tofino are living a happy, uncomplicated life. They live to play, live to surf, live for days of friends, parties, pay cheques, regular physical activity, and carnality. On a morning like today, as a bunch of surfers talk, talk, talk waves, waves, waves, you've got to wonder — crisis? What crisis?

Meanwhile back at the Legion, all sorts of Hawaiian kitsch is being set up on stage for the night's festivities. The Legion Luau scene may be as Hawaiian as a hula hoop but it does act as a nod of respect to surfing's ancestors.

According to Hawaiian legend, canoes, livestock and even land were wagered on a single ride through the surf. So today in Tofino, during the Surf Jam competition, where surfers are competing for small prize money to benefit the British Columbia Surfing Association (BCSA), the idea of competition seems a natural extension of Hawaiian history. That doesn't stop some local surfers from muttering about the commercialization of the sport

Poster from the Summer Surf Jam, 2000.

and questioning, once again, whether surfing is "really" a sport or a way of life.

Jenny Hudnall teaches surf lessons through her company Surf Sister, which she established in 1999 exclusively for women. As for competition, Hudnall says she has "mixed feelings for sure." She helped start BCSA to get kids involved in competitive surfing and to make it possible for kids to get community funding to travel and surf. "Nobody really had the money to go down to California or to fly in for contests," she says.

The Tofino contests, which began in 1993, had twenty-five or thirty entrants. "There were always three girls," Hudnall says. "It was pretty much pointless to go in the contest because we knew that Katherine Bruhwiler was going to get first, I was going to get second, and Cathy Temple was going to get third. It was like that forever. I think I beat Katherine one time, up until about 1996."

The BC Surfing Association was formed to represent west coast surfers. There was a whole east coast Canadian contingent that started their surfing association first. "They wanted to send all their guys to the World contest and we were like, 'Hey, we've got really good surfers and you guys surf like crap compared to the west coast.' And you can quote me on that too," says Hudnall, heatedly.

The Tofino contests, held every two years to co-ordinate with the World Surfing Games (sponsored by the International Surfing Association) are getting bigger and attracting more sponsorship. "The more advertising surfing gets, the more mainstream it is, the more sponsors we get for the contests, and the more money," says Hudnall. "The events are well organized and everybody is totally supportive, but I kind of wish there was more local support for it. It's run by people from out of town, just a bunch of people coming to Tofino, setting up camp and running the show because they know how to do it. They have the time, the energy and the money to spend on it, whereas people here are either too flaky to get it together, or they just don't know how it really works, or they can't hold up to the expectations of everybody from the city. It takes a lot of organization."

In a way, the Surf Jam competition is a throwback to Ralph Devries' days of surfing, when he would surf in clear view of the bar at the Wickanninish Inn. In fact the first surf contest to take place in BC was held in front of the Inn in 1966. The event was watched by close to 2,000 spectators who were treated to a salmon bake on the beach. In Ucluelet, a surf stomp and a seafood feast were held as part of the festivities.

"I always had quite an audience when I surfed and I liked that. It pushed me a little bit more," says Devries. "I mentioned that to my son, Peter, and he said he felt the same way."

At the age of fourteen, Peter Devries got his first sponsor — Storm Surf Shop in Tofino, which is run by Allister Fernie and is doing very nicely, thank you very much. More recently Hurley International, a clothing and wetsuit manufacturer based in California and recently bought out by Nike, started bringing Peter down to California to surf in contests there, paying his entrance fee and providing him with accommodation. When he was seventeen, he represented Canada at the World Surfing Games in Brazil. And in front of a hometown crowd in Tofino, he had his first big surfing victory when he won the Quiksilver/Roxy Summer Surf Jam 2000, finishing just ahead of his Chesterman Beach neighbours, Sepp and Raph Bruhwiler.

Despite Peter Devries' win, making surfing your career is

tough because there isn't really any money in it. "Doing these contests is one way of bringing in money," says Hudnall. "If you get sponsorship, you get all your gear paid for. It's expensive to pay for the gear. That way you don't have to work another job to pay for all your surf gear. Your whole world is surfing and for some people that's what they love. That's what I'm doing right now and I love it."

When the younger Sadlers began surfing they received help from older surfers. "When we started out there was a strong contingent of older surfers and, because there were fewer of us coming up in the ranks, they had a chance to help us out. To point out etiquette, to point out how to use rip currents, how to look at the water and see things, knowing how to read waves. And I think that is a huge advantage to the person just starting out," recalls Harold.

With the increased commercialization of surfing in the last few years, lessons have filled that gap. Live to Surf, established in 1984, was the first board rental service in Tofino since the 1960s. It was owned by Liz Zed and run by a group of women, including Jenny Hudnall. "Guys from Vancouver would come in, like, super cool surfer dudes and put their wetsuits on backwards, and we would just crack up. Send a guy bright red back to the change room. We had fun with it," recalls Jenny.

Concerned moms also came into the shop. They wanted lessons for their kids, but they also wanted to make sure they were safe — taught all about the waves and taken to the right beach. "I decided, we could make some money at this," says Hudnall who charged $25 for a surf lesson. "I made up these signs that read: 'Surf Lessons Taught by Members of the Canadian National Surf Team.' That was in '93 when we were just getting the BC Surfing Association together," she adds. "I put up posters with a little picture of a wave and my phone number, and I did lessons. Raph did lessons. So did Katherine and Sepp. We all did a few here and there during the summer and it worked. We were all making money at it for a while."

In 1998 the Surf Divas, a group of female surfers from California, came to Tofino to give lessons to women. Their clinics were sold out. The idea caught on with Jenny Hudnall. "It was like, click!" says Hudnall. "Let's do the all-girls thing. Forget the just-surf-lessons surf school, let's do just girls. Because it was so cool the way they taught it. And the girls that took the class were just so stoked. I decided that's what I wanted to do. And that's exactly how Surf Sister came about."

The summer of 1999 was the first year for Surf Sister, and business was good. The first clinic was full. "That was pretty much word of mouth because I didn't have any of the advertising together. I didn't know how to start a business — I'm still learning here. Then we got the website up and running."

As Hudnall points out, however, attempts at making surfing into a business in this neck of the woods started way before her. "My dad and Bruce Atkey, a true local soul-surfer guy, started a surf school at Long Beach in the '60s," she says. "My dad bought out a surf shop in California that was going out of business and he and Bruce brought up all the longboards and wetsuits to Long Beach and they set up a surf shop where the Park Warden's office is now. That's what my mom says anyway. She told us last night, and I couldn't believe it because he's telling everybody you can't make money from surfing. And I'm like, 'Wait a second, this doesn't quite fit.' I find it quite interesting to see that they tried to make it happen when they were my age, but it didn't take off because it wasn't as mainstream as it is now. And now it just seems to work. Our generation is just taking to it, and it's only natural because everything grows."

When she was growing up, Hudnall lived part of the year with her father, Jim, in California — Del Mar, La Jolla and Santa Cruz — and the rest of the year in Tofino. "We thought we were so cool," she says of her exposure to California's surf culture. "Because I was from California basically everyone was like 'Oh you're the California girl.' Even though I was born here, I brought back that surf culture, the clothes and the stickers, and the cool surfy stuff. So it was basically that connection with California, where we knew it was cool down there and we were bringing that coolness to Tofino."

Jim Hudnall was a product of the golden age of modern surfing in the late 1950s. From 1907 and its introduction at Huntington Beach, to its boom during the late 1950s, surfing in California was considered to have experienced a period of Eden-like "innocence." In the early 1950's, in California, the entire surfing population consisted of maybe a few hundred people, and most of them were riding redwood boards, paddleboards, or balsa / red-woods. Within a few years surfing had become so popular that board manufactures began popping up. All along the Southern California coast, from Santa Barbara to San Diego, thousands of gremmies — green surfers — took to the waves and beaches like never before.

In British Columbia, the start of the surfing boom dates back to the mid-1990s, although for some that was too soon.

"Blaming certain people for exposing surfing I don't really think is a good thing," says Jenny Hudnall. "I think a lot of people become bitter about surfing because it has become popular and it has gotten crowded. I could imagine it if I'd been surfing for the last thirty years and seen it go from no people to what it is today — it's like watching roads go from horses to cars."

The current growth of surfing in Tofino doesn't seem to faze the Sadlers. "I see the same excitement in their faces as I had when I was a kid," says Harold, who took part in the longboard competition at Surf Jam. "It only ticks me off if I can't park in the Cox Bay parking lot because it's full and I want to check the surf. But other than that it hasn't changed a whole lot. What has changed is the number of core guys that live here. There are a lot more good surfers. Ten years ago we could paddle out to any good break. I didn't care how many people were out there, we could get our waves. I'd put my elbows up and go out there. It was just a matter of seniority and pecking order. Frankly, we could paddle harder and faster than anybody else. We earned it. That ain't the case anymore. The fact is that some of these guys are now pad-dling deeper than we are. They are better than we are. They're younger."

There's also the changes in boards and wetsuits. "Their equip-ment is so good," adds Ken.

"That's the one thing I'd change," jokes Harold. "I'd make every one of those buggers surf on some half-water-logged piece of equipment for five years and wear a beaver tail wetsuit for a while. See how they'd like that!"

Competition is fine by the Sadlers, with some reservations. "As long as it doesn't become the sole purpose for doing what you are doing," says Harold. "The competitions are fun but it is all about the moment. And anyway, being the best surfer isn't about winning competitions. It's about people having the most fun. Whether we like it or not, these surf contests are put on for promotional purposes. A lot of the young guys now have a sponsorship. When I was growing up that was unheard of."

"Now that tells you that, A, there is a market; B, there is some exposure, and C, these guys are good," says Ken. "A perfect example is the winner of the longboard competition at Surf Jam. He'd just come back from the Worlds in Brazil, and when he made his acceptance speech for the trophy and the money, it was very professional. He thanked the sponsors who had backed him and so on. You could see the professionalism of it, whereas in times past the surfing contests we had were just strictly for fun. But ultimately, I don't see the contests changing things."

So, a luau at the Legion? Sure. Why not?

Surfing is the message in a bottle of global culture, from the ancients of Polynesia, Captain Cook, the Tla-o-qui-aht, California, and now here to the Clayoquot Legion, looking out at Opitsaht, where today's cedar surfers are partying. The world has gotten smaller, and Tofino is no longer at the end of the road; it's at the end of the block. With a million visitors coming to Tofino each year, the world has come to Tofino. The one-turntable-world that supplies the ambient beats on the beach during the competition, the nods to Hawaii, the annual trips many of Tofino's younger surfers take to Costa Rica, Mexico, Samoa, and Hawaii emphasize the global nature of the sport. It accounts for the transnational beats that wash in with the waves during the Summer Surf Jam competition.

Paddling Out

In October, 1996 BC Parks arrived at Sombrio Beach with notices in hand. "Effective January 31, 1997," they read, "all persons are to vacate residences within Juan de Fuca Provincial Park."

The government hired a crew of unemployed loggers to haul out cabins by truck and helicopter. The "Sombrio Nation," as it had been dubbed, disappeared virtually overnight. The Oke-Johnsons moved to Port Renfrew twenty kilometres farther north. Steve Johnson worked splitting cedar shakes for a living. On a good day he made $160 for four hours' work, not including the four-wheel drive to the middle of a clearcut somewhere near Port Renfrew. It was a little hard on Steve's fifty-year-old body, which had started to give him some trouble. He figured his knee pain came from turning left on the waves at Sombrio for so many years. He also developed skin cancer.

Barbara Oke missed the social life of the beach. "People don't just drop in," she said. "I remember one day thinking, what's different about this place is that nobody is coming to knock on the door. At Sombrio there were always people coming to visit and here they don't."

Port Renfrew is a raw, rough, logger town that has an-end-of-the-road feel; it serves as the end of the Pacific Coast trail. Sooke, sixty kilometres to the south, is the closest place for fuel. The only food store in town has all the charm of a military canteen. It exists for one reason: booze. While Tofino evolves into an eco-adven-

Out of the woods and into the water. PHOTO COURTESY BRIAN HOWELL

ture playground for the wealthy, Port Renfrew's charm, if it could be called that, is its complete lack of desire to bend over for the tourists.

Drive straight though town and you'll arrive at the Port Renfrew Hotel. Built in the 1920s, the clapboard facing, porch overhang and horse-tie railings suggest a wild-west town. Parked out front are a couple of pick-up trucks with dogs in the back, and inside the hotel is an assortment of fellows with ball caps and Stanfield fisherman sweaters. Just out the door from the hotel is a long wharf.

On Februauy 20, 2000, Jesse drove a truck onto the wharf. The last words his brother Isaiah said to him were, "Don't drive off the dock!"

Jesse drove off the dock. His two passengers survived, but Jesse did not. "Jesse was an old soul," says Barbara. "He was solidly grounded. He was curious. It was great that he grew up on the beach and didn't go to school. We encouraged him and all the children to be curious. To think about this wonder they were surrounded with, the sun, moon and stars. The sand and the waves.

Jesse had a deep sense of wonder and he was always so positive. He was capable of learning whatever he took up. The only thing I wish he learned was to drive better," says Barbara, mournfully.

In the accident, Jesse's surfboard ended up in the water. Two weeks later it washed ashore in the Queen Charlottes. The person who found the board called the dealer in Sooke and was told it belonged to Jesse. "Jesse is King" can still be seen on bumper stickers and graffiti up and down the cedar surf, and there is now a locked gate at the end of the wharf, a gate that had been talked about for years.

Unfortunately, Jesse's death would not be the end of Barbara Oke's troubles. Within three months of Jesse's death, two more of her children would die in separate motor vehicle accidents, and in January 2002, Steve Johnson succumbed to a brain tumour, a consequence of the skin cancer he was suffering from.

It is hard not to reach some paradise-lost conclusions about the Oke-Johnsons' fortunes since leaving Sombrio and its beach paradise. But Barbara isn't sure. "Is there a relationship between our leaving and the accidents?" she asks. "Will the accidents continue because we left? I don't know." One thing Barbara is clear on is that she plans on putting up a shelter at Sombrio this spring. She is vague on plans to live there.

As for myself, I think of Leah sitting it out in Port Renfrew during the summer of her youth. In this end-of-the-road town, you get a feel for what is available to her in the absence of the opportunity to make a go of it in the wide world of surfing. The week after Jesse died, Leah qualified for the World Championships in Brazil at a BCSA surfing meet held in Tofino in honour of Jesse Oke.

In the spring of 2002, Billy Leach was forced to close his Island Rhino surfboard shop in Ucluelet due to a lack of funds. While the surf economy pounds the shores of Tofino, Ucluelet, thirty kilometres down the road, still tries to find its foothold. Tofino and Ucluelet share the only six-kilometre stretch of sand in Canada near a road. Shouldn't they both be doing well? Maybe Ucluelet should have a luau at *its* Legion?

Is there a meaning to surfing, other than it's fun and that you can't fake it, that there is a power greater than us, and that power is a wave, and that wave is God?

It's hard to say. But some of the changes over time in the sport in BC are clear: the disappearance of surf-squat communities; the emergence of elders in the sport; increased participation by women; the transformation of Tofino from a remote resource-based town to one that is visited by a million people each year and with an economy capable of supporting several surf shops, surf schools and the annual surf competitions; and the growth of competitive surfing in BC. Surfing's growing popularity will also bring an end to the primal instinct of territorialism: how long you surfed a spot won't matter to a new generation, who will have to sort out for themselves how to get along in the water.

The crossover of snowboarders and skateboarders, which has increased the popularity of the sport, and the development of regional surfing family "dynasties" including the Sadlers, the Bruhwillers, the Oke-Johnsons, the Atkeys, the Devries, and the Hudnalls are two other aspects of the evolution of surfing in BC. Whether the sport will continue to grow, or a lot of dusty surf-boards will start to accumulate in people's garages in this province is difficult to say. But the thrill of surfing remains clear.

I watch as three surfers stride into the gaping expanse of the ocean and liquid-blue sky; they are grinning, "stoked." The white streamers of frothing foam acts like vines dragging them in. Their footsteps in the sand disappear with an oncoming wave. They look tiny, almost foolish when, laughing, they physically cast themselves against the very physical, ever-shifting landscape. They walk out as far as possible through the waves crumbling into the shoreline before going belly down on their boards. Arms reaching out towards the horizon, they begin paddling out.

A Surfing Glossary

aerial airborne manoeuvre

air getting airborne

amped charged up; stoked; fired

backdoor to pull into a tube from behind the peak

backwash flood of water returning off the foreshore against incoming waves

bail to abandon a board; to jump off, usually without regard to the board's future

bake a closeout

bashing body surfing

beach breaks waves formed over sand and sandbars; can shift seasonally, and from storm to storm

bodyboard aka boogie board, sponge; a paipoboard modified in 1971 by Tom Morey and used to ride dangerous shallow reefs safely; lay prone and augment with swim fins

bonzer in Australia, bonzer is equivalent slang for "bitchen": the Campbell brothers of Southern California adopted the term in the 1970s to describe their five-fin surf board

boost getting airborne off the lip

brah from "bruddah," Hawaiian pidgin for brother

bro a buddy or friend

bucket helmet

bump a swell

bumps the build-up of wax on a surfboard deck

cant   angling the outside fins towards the rail so that the inner angle is ninety degrees or more. Cant really puts the fin in a place where it needs to be. For example, when you are doing a bottom turn, the inside fin is angled more towards the rail and is in a better position to hold the board in, especially when you have one or more fins out of the water. Cant makes the board handle better on its rails

carve   symmetrical, fluid turns

channel   a deeper area where excess water, piled up by waves, flows out to sea

cheater five   five toes on the nose. Keep your weight back on the board to maintain trim and speed, squat down and extend one foot forward

clean   waves with unrippled faces; usually offshore or in no wind

clucked   afraid; intimidated by the wave

cnoid waves   As waves come into shallow water their shapes change to something called "cnoids" which have short, steep crests and a long, shallow troughs, resembling lines of corduroy

concave   soft chine indentation running lengthways on the bottom of a board; believed to create lift

crew   a group of surfers defined by break or area

dogging   going backside in the pit

down rail   the deck curves down to meet the flat bottom at a hard edge

drop in late   catching the steepest part of a wave

drop   as in dropping from the crest of the wave to the pit

dropping in   catching a wave that is already occupied; taking off on the shoulder while someone is taking off deeper

dune   a big, peaky wave

egg   refers to the slow rounded shape of a nose, tail or rail

face   clean, smooth wall on the shore side of a wave

falls   top of the wave pitches out and throws a waterfall shoreward

fan   a fan of spray off a turn like one a water skier throws

fetch   determines the size of a wave: wind speed x time x distance

fish   shortboard with added width and thickness; designed to

improve wave catching capability while maintaining performance; a shorboard for small conditions

flick nose   an increase in the rate of rocker near the nose

fluff   spray off the lip

frequency downshifting   the increase of wave period within a
fetch; a decrease in frequency is an increase in period

frigged   snaked

fully/full on   with commitment and intensity

fun board   mid-sized board designed for ease of ride in small
conditions

gash   very sharp turn

gnarly   awesome and intimidating

going off   a break under optimum conditions

gouge   sharp, fast turn

green room   inside a full cover-up tube

grem or *gremmie*   short for gremlin; 1960s' American term for
young (possibly mischievous) surfer or pre-adolescent surfer

grommet   adolescent surfer

ground swells   waves formed over vast distances; well-formed
and powerful "mackers"

gun   or rhino; a board for big waves. It is long, narrow, and
pointy both at the nose and the tail for maximum rail contact.
Usually thick and heavy and ranging in length from 7 to 10
feet; AKA "elephant gun" or "rhino chaser"; so named because
you take it with you when you are hunting big game

gunned   undergunned or overgunned refers to the size of a
board in relation to wave conditions

hard rail   sharper edge to grab a wave

hiddie   from hideous, intense

hoot   howling and yelping approval and encouragement to
buddies

impact zone   the point where the waves break for the first time

inside   where waves continue to break, reform, and break again
if they're big enough

jag   retreat after getting worked

kneeboard   aka kneelo

leash   a line attaching the board to the surfer's ankle (for a
shortboard), to the calf just below the knee (longboard), or to
the wrist (bodyboard). Before the mid-1970s, we used surgical

rubber tubing. Modern leashes have little elastic property, in-line swivels to prevent fouling, and optional quick-release pins at the ankle

line-up   just beyond the impact zone where you wait to catch waves

lip   curling lip at the top of a wave

log or stick   slang for surf board

longboard   Longboards are usually over 9 feet long. Because of their size they are easier to paddle and you can get into waves sooner. On the downside, they are less manoeuvrable and can get pretty unwieldy in steep waves

mal   a longboard most places except America

mini-mal   mid-sized board with longboard characteristics

nipped   nipples rubbed raw by board or suit

noodle   exhausted, overall condition, or specific as in noodle armed

outside   offshore; beyond where the waves break

paipoboard   wooden Hawaiian bodyboard

pearl   to go "pearl diving"; the nose of a board submerges and usually the wave pushes the rest of the board over the nose, and the surfer along with it

period   time between waves. The energy / power of a wave is proportional not only to its height but its period

pin tail   pointed tail; aids in stability of board

pit   the hollowest portion of a breaking wave

pitch   the act of the lip throwing out in front of the wave

pitch   throw; angle of any run to rise

pitted   being in the pit of the wave

point breaks   waves formed in reaction to the land form; consistent

pop   kickout

poser   a non-surfer playing the role of a surfer

pucker factor   the effect an intimidating wave has on one's ability to remain relaxed

puff   a spitting wave

pumping   large swell

quad   four-fin board; two normal-sized fins with two smaller fins in line behind them *quiver*   a surfer's collection of boards; a board bag that holds several boards

rail   side edge of a board

reef breaks   waves formed over an underwater reef or rock; consistent

reverse "V"   hard chine protruding ridge running lengthways on the bottom of a board

rip   to surf to the height of one's abilities

river mouth breaks   waves created by the sediments deposited at a river's mouth, similar to beach breaks but sometimes more susceptible to change

rocker   the arc of the tail that bends up; more rocker means easier turning and less speed

room   inside a large barrel

scab   a reef or rock

scabbed   getting damaged by a reef or rock

schlong   thick, long, old-style single-fin surfboard

section   any appreciable length of wave that has common characteristics and timing

sectiony   breaking in sections

shore-dump / soup / slop   unorganized sloppy foam; no good for nothing

shortboard   the most common surfboard. They range in length from 5 to 7½ feet and tend to be used for high-performance, contest-style surfing. Shortboards usually have pointed noses and three fins, although other configurations are common. A shortboard sacrifices paddling and floatation for the sake of performance

shred   ability to execute rapid repeated turns; a shortboard term

sick   excellent, top notch; describing a surfer, stunt, manoeuvre, or conditions

sideslip   when your board stops tracking forwards and moves sideways

sine waves   in deep water, swells are very well approximated by pure sine waves

skimboards   glassed plywood disc or oval for riding shallow beaches at the water's edge; run, throw it down, hop on

slam   bounce off the lip as it begins to pitch

slash   cutback

snake   paddling around behind someone who is in position and stealing their wave. In effect, the snake is taking ownership of the wave by being the closest rider to its breaking portion.

soft rail   rounder edge so the board is looser

spoon   concave in the underside nose of a longboard; increases lift for nose riding

square tail   with the introduction of multi fins, it became advantageous to loosen up the board with a clean-profile tail design

squash tail   wide, rounded tail; introduced after the advent of advanced fin systems to loosen up boards

squid   unlikeable individual

steep   refers to the angle or the pitch of a wave face

stink-eye   hard, cold, menacing stare

stoked   geared up; wound up; full of enthusiasm

stuffed   getting driven under the water by a wave coming down on you

stylie   with good form; with grace

surfer's knots   large bumps on the tops of feet and on knees caused by callusing where one continuously contacts a board

swallow tail   double-pointed tail with an indentation in the centre; functional on single-fin boards; aids in the holding characteristics of the board

swish   a meek or fearful surfer

tail kick   an increase in the rate of rocker near the tail

tanker   longboard

thrashed   the action a wave plays on you. It feels like being in a large washing machine

throwing tail   sliding the tail in a turn; breaking the grip of the fins

thruster   three similar-sized fins

toe-in   pushing the front of the fins in. On some boards, they would put the toe so that a string from the nose of the board to the fin was the alignment for the fins toe-in. Of course this represents a lot of toe-in! Toe-in causes pressure on the outside of the fins to be greater than on the inside, thereby making the board want to swivel to either side with a little surfer input. It eliminated tracking on the earlier twin fins, and made for a looser, more responsive board

tow-ins   getting towed into waves that are too large to paddle into

tri-fin   three-fin board; one large and two smaller fins

trim   adjusting your position on a board so that it planes and achieves its maximum speed

tube   the cylindrical or cone-shaped hole created when the lip pitches out far and clean enough to create a space between the wave and the falls

twin   two-fin board

twinzer   four-fin board; two normal-sized fins with two smaller fins mirrored a few inches outside and forward of them

vertical   turn straight up the wave

waffling   rapidly working the board back and forth

wannabe   someone who wants to be a surfer

wax   paraffin + colour + scent + additives to make it apply at specific temperatures; used on deck of boards for traction

wind swells   waves formed close to the shore by local wind conditions; unorganized with a tendency to be slop

wipe out   a fall, particularly a spectacular fall

Bibliography

Arima, E.Y. "A Report on a West Coast Whaling Canoe Reconstructed at Port Renfrew, B.C." *History and Archaelogy 5*. National Historical Parks and Sites Branch, Parks Canada, Department of Indian and Northern Affairs, Ottawa, 1974.

Butt, Tony. "Heavy Water Cold Hold-Downs." *The Surfer's Path* (December / January 2002).

Dufour, Pat. "Survivor Signs Himself Out: I Knew I Could Last." *The Times-Colonist* (December 29, 1974): Section 2, page 15.

Harper, Frank. "The Forest at Opitsaht." *The Sound Newspaper*, 1990.

Mallin, Lorne. "Our Surf's Up: For Your Leisure Try the Island's Waves." *Vancouver Sun* (June 10, 1966), Leisure Section, p. 3.

Koppel, Tom. *Kanaka: The Untold Story of Hawaiian Pioneers in BC and the Pacific Northwest*. Vancouver: Whitecap Books, 1995.

Marcus, Ben. "From Polynesia With Love: The History of Surfing from Captain Cook to the Present." www.surfingforlife.com (March 31, 2003).

Sproat, Malcolm Gilbert. "The Nootka: Scenes and Studies of Savage Life," in *West Coast Heritage Series*, edited by Charles Lillard. Victoria, BC: Sono Nis Press, 1987.

Trower, Peter. "From the Hill to the Spill." *Raincoast Chronicle First Five*. Vancouver: Harbour Publishing, 1976.

www.coastalbc.com

Young, Nat. *History of Surfing*. B&G Enterprises, 1998.

TRANSMONTANUS is edited by Terry Glavin. Editorial correspondence should be sent to Transmontanus, PO Box C25, Fernhill Road, Mayne Island, BC VON 2J0.

New Star Books Ltd.
107 - 3477 Commercial Street
Vancouver, BC
V5N 4E8
www.NewStarBooks.com
info@NewStarBooks.com

Edited for press by Melva McLean
Cover by Rayola Graphic Design
Cover photos by Jeremy Koreski
Map by Eric Leinberger
Typesetting by New Star Books
Printed & bound in Canada by AGMV Marquis
First printing June 2003

Publication of this work is made possible by grants from the Canada Council, the British Columbia Arts Council, and the Department of Canadian Heritage Book Publishing Industry Development Program.

NATIONAL LIBRARY OF CANADA CATALOGUING IN PUBLICATION DATA

Shilling, Grant
  The cedar surf : an informal history of surfing in British Columbia / Grant Shilling.

(Transmontanus 1200-3336 10)
Includes bibliographical references.
ISBN 0-921586-93-0

  1. Surfing — British Columbia — History.   I. Title.   II. Series.
GV840.S82B74 2003   797.3'2'09711   C2003-910648-9